T0277123

Cambridge Elements ≡

Elements in Bioethics and Neuroethics
edited by
Thomasine Kushner
California Pacific Medical Center, San Francisco

EUTHANASIA AS PRIVILEGED COMPASSION

Martin Buijsen
Erasmus University Rotterdam

CAMBRIDGE
UNIVERSITY PRESS

CAMBRIDGE
UNIVERSITY PRESS

Shaftesbury Road, Cambridge CB2 8EA, United Kingdom

One Liberty Plaza, 20th Floor, New York, NY 10006, USA

477 Williamstown Road, Port Melbourne, VIC 3207, Australia

314–321, 3rd Floor, Plot 3, Splendor Forum, Jasola District Centre,
New Delhi – 110025, India

103 Penang Road, #05–06/07, Visioncrest Commercial, Singapore 238467

Cambridge University Press is part of Cambridge University Press & Assessment,
a department of the University of Cambridge.

We share the University's mission to contribute to society through the pursuit of
education, learning and research at the highest international levels of excellence.

www.cambridge.org
Information on this title: www.cambridge.org/9781009517607

DOI: 10.1017/9781009086844

First published 2024

A catalogue record for this publication is available from the British Library.

ISBN 978-1-009-51760-7 Hardback
ISBN 978-1-009-07817-7 Paperback
ISSN 2752-3934 (online)
ISSN 2752-3926 (print)

Euthanasia as Privileged Compassion

Elements in Bioethics and Neuroethics

DOI: 10.1017/9781009086844
First published online: May 2024

Martin Buijsen
Erasmus University Rotterdam

Author for correspondence: Martin Buijsen, buijsen@law.eur.nl

Abstract: This Element overviews developments and issues in Dutch euthanasia practice. Following an outline of the history of the Dutch Euthanasia Act and a survey of the most critical trends and figures, some current issues are explored in depth: euthanasia and incompetency, euthanasia by nonphysicians, and euthanasia for those who consider their lives completed. This Element is intended for a general readership, including undergraduate students in law, medicine, or ethics. This title is also available as Open Access on Cambridge Core.

This Element also has a video abstract: www.cambridge.org/Buijsen

Keywords: euthanasia, compassion, autonomy, completed life, physician-assisted suicide

ISBNs: 9781009517607 (HB), 9781009078177 (PB), 9781009086844 (OC)
ISSNs: 2752-3934 (online), 2752-3926 (print)

Contents

Preface

Euthanasia is a controversial subject. Although the number of countries in which it is practiced is increasing, the Netherlands is still one of relatively few where it is allowed. In the Netherlands, euthanasia is permitted, provided certain very specific requirements are met. However, Dutch euthanasia policy and practice do give rise to various misunderstandings, which I will address in this Element. My main objective is to clarify.

Although the Netherlands is not the only country to have decriminalized euthanasia to a considerable extent, it does have the most experience in this area. In that respect, the Netherlands is unique. Because of the way it is regulated, the wealth of knowledge of the practice is overwhelming. Opponents of legalizing euthanasia usually have little regard for the benefits of transparency and the safeguards it provides. Because of its long-standing tradition, the Netherlands has also experienced (and is experiencing!) unique developments. Proponents of legalizing euthanasia tend to have a blind spot for the problematic aspects of some of those developments.

Euthanasia evokes strong moral sentiments as well. This Element is not an ethical pamphlet. I do not advocate the legalization of euthanasia nor make a plea for its criminalization. Although the Element aims, first and foremost, to inform the reader about how euthanasia as a practice has grown in the Netherlands and the direction it is taking, it is certainly not devoid of critical commentary.

Since the Dutch Euthanasia Act came into force on April 1, 2002, I have closely observed developments. I have written about many of them in articles that have appeared in academic and professional journals, as well as news-papers. This Element allows me to reflect on my earlier writings, sharpen my thoughts, and develop a comprehensive view of Dutch euthanasia policy, the direction in which the practice is evolving, and its challenges.

And finally, the chosen perspective of this Element may appear predominantly legal. Although I have taken great pains to avoid legal jargon, it must not be forgotten that the Dutch euthanasia policy came about by case law. Current issues are subject to judicial scrutiny as well. The story of euthanasia in the Netherlands simply cannot be told without referring extensively to law.

1 The Euthanasia Act and Its Genesis

To properly understand Dutch euthanasia practice, it is imperative to know how it came about. Numerous parties have contributed to the Dutch notion of euthanasia, but least of all the legislator. The genesis of the practice can best be described as a growing consensus among societal stakeholders on what counts as standard medicine and what as nonstandard medicine at the end of life.[1] Euthanasia is a broad term that can be (and is) used to refer to a range of end-of-life practices. The Dutch understanding of euthanasia is very specific. It is important to realize up front that practices that could also be qualified as euthanasia, and might elsewhere pass for euthanasia, are considered standard medicine in the Netherlands (Section 1.5).

1.1 Before 1969

The Euthanasia Act (officially: the Act on the Assessment of Termination of Life on Request and Assistance in Suicide) came into force on April 1, 2002. Its enactment formally concluded a development that had begun many years before. As early as 1984, all the building blocks provided fell into place, making way for the practice as we know it today.

Until the 1960s, hardly any writings on euthanasia were published in the Netherlands. Although termination of life on request and assistance in suicide had been included as crimes in the Dutch Criminal Code since it came into force in 1886, no prosecution of these offenses took place until 1944. It was not until that year that the Supreme Court of the Netherlands issued a judgment in which euthanasia was the subject of dispute; but because the Supreme Court only dwelt on the duty of the criminal court to substantiate its decision, this ruling is generally not considered the first one on euthanasia in the Netherlands.[2]

In the so-called Eindhoven doctor case (1952), a sanatorium resident suffering severely from tuberculosis had repeatedly urged his brother – a physician – to end his life. The brother had finally complied by giving him Codinovo tablets and administering morphine in lethal doses. In court, he argued, inter alia, that he had no choice but to follow the voice of his conscience. In its judgment, upheld by the appellate court, the District Court ruled that no extralegal ground for impunity exists according to which a person may take another person's life following the voice of their conscience, not even when this person is suffering severely and explicitly requests that they wish their life to be ended. The brother was sentenced to a suspended prison term of one year.[3]

This was the first time a Dutch court ruled on a doctor's deliberate termination of life at the request of a patient who – in his own words – was suffering "almost unbearably." But there was no proper doctor–patient relationship, and even in the medical profession, the physician's actions were primarily seen as those of a brother.[4]

1.2 1969–2002

The change in mentality in the 1960s, characterized by secularization, emanci-pation, and increasing individualism, also made itself felt in the relationship between physicians and their patients. That decade saw the birth of the Dutch patients' rights movement. Physicians' authority met with challenges, and respect for the patient's autonomy was claimed; this was later translated into legally enforceable rights regarding information, consent, surrogate decision-making, and so on.[5]

The 1960s were also a time of significant medical–technological progress, which raised new moral questions. Medical techniques made it possible to preserve life, even when recovery is no longer possible. Of considerable influence on Dutch understanding of euthanasia was the publication in 1969 of a booklet entitled *Medical Power and Medical Ethics*, written by physician, psychiatrist, and philosopher Jan Hendrik van den Berg.[6] The first edition caused a stir because of its plea for an ethics that no longer acknowledged the duty to preserve life unconditionally. "Physicians are duty-bound to preserve, spare, and prolong human life wherever and whenever that is meaningful," claimed the author.[7] But if it is no longer meaningful, he argued, they have the moral right to end their patients' lives, passively or actively.[8] In the Netherlands, Van den Berg is credited with firmly putting the topic of euthanasia on the public agenda, where it has remained ever since.

1.2.1 Postma (1973)

A family relationship also featured in the Postma case. The patient, a severely ill seventy-eight-year-old nursing home resident, was, among other things, partially paralyzed and incontinent, but mentally still quick-witted. A month before her death, she contracted pneumonia, intensely longed for death, and urged her physician and family members to end her life. The doctor was convinced of the severity of her suffering but thought he could not proceed to actively end her life due to the criminal prohibition of termination of life on request. In addition, he feared resistance from the nursing home staff. The patient's daughter, Mrs. Postma-van Boven, who happened to be a physician, ultimately administered a lethal morphine injection to her mother. She was sentenced by the District Court to only one week's suspended imprisonment "given the utter purity of her motives."[9]

The Postma case was a milestone because, for the first time, a court considered the possibility of impunity for termination of life on request. The District Court put the question of whether an exception to the ban could be justified to a physician, a healthcare inspector. In his expert opinion, several due care requirements of the later Euthanasia Act were clearly recognizable. He considered an exception to the ban conceivable if the following criteria were met:

- The patient is incurably ill because of a disease or an accident or is medically considered as such.
- The physical or mental suffering is subjectively unbearable or severe for the patient.

- The patient has expressed a wish to end their life or, in any case, to be relieved of their suffering, if need be, in advance in writing.
- The euthanasia is performed by a physician: either the attending physician or another in consultation with that physician.[10]

According to the inspector, the patient would also have to be in the process of dying, or the start of that process would have to be imminent.[11] The judges did not accept that requirement.[12] Nor is it mentioned in the Euthanasia Act.

The physician's appeal to *force majeure* was rejected because she had not first tried to alleviate her mother's suffering. Unlike the rulings in the Eindhoven doctor case, this verdict caused much public controversy. Times had clearly changed. The court case resulted in numerous publications on end-of-life decision-making. It also triggered the creation of advocacy organizations committed to the social acceptance and legalization of euthanasia.[13]

1.2.2 Wertheim (1981)

Another important court decision was made in the Wertheim case, involving a euthanasia activist (Mrs. Wertheim-Elink Schuurman) who had assisted another woman in suicide. At the latter's request, she provided a lethal drug, which resulted in the woman's death. Her life had been a series of tragedies. She was an alcoholic, lived in isolation, and thought she had cancer, which a later autopsy revealed she did not.

The District Court considered, inter alia, that "according to many nowadays – in contrast to the time when the Criminal Code was drafted – suicide is not necessarily unacceptable in exceptional cases,"[14] and referred to the criteria mentioned in the Postma ruling. These were strengthened by the Court's explicit acknowledgment that the request for assisted suicide must be voluntary, well-considered, and sustained, that there are no other options available to improve the situation and that the decision to end life was made after the person concerned was fully informed about this. The Court added that a physician must be involved in deciding whether to assist in suicide.[15] Again, these were requirements that ended up in the Euthanasia Act.

Because most of the requirements had not been met, Mrs. Wertheim's appeal to *force majeure* in the sense of emergency was unsuccessful. She was sentenced to a suspended prison term of six months with a probation period of one year.[16]

After the Wertheim ruling, the Procurators General decided that every case of termination of life on request or assisted suicide that would become known to the Public Prosecutor's Office should be referred to them for a prosecution decision.[17] Such a decision was made in the Schoonheim case (1984), in which the Supreme Court's ruling more or less definitively shaped Dutch euthanasia policy.[18]

1.2.3 Schoonheim (1984)

The patient was a ninety-five-year-old woman, permanently disabled, bedridden, and entirely dependent on others for her care. She had written an advance directive requesting euthanasia, was still fully competent, and, as her condition deteriorated, asked ever more pressingly for her life to be ended. After a severe breakdown, leaving her unconscious for days and unable to eat or drink, she again insisted on euthanasia to avoid a repeat of the horrible experience. According to Dr. Schoonheim, her family doctor, she found the experiences of everyday life extremely burdensome, causing her to suffer unbearably.

After consulting a junior doctor, the general practitioner decided to comply with his patient's wishes, whereupon he was prosecuted. Although the charges were initially dismissed,[19] Dr. Schoonheim was nevertheless found guilty on appeal.[20] Although no penalty was imposed, he appealed to the Supreme Court, arguing that the appellate court had not sufficiently addressed whether the patient's suffering was so unbearable that the doctor reasonably had no choice but to spare her that suffering by euthanasia. With respect to this point, the judges sympathized with Dr. Schoonheim. The Supreme Court considered that a physician could successfully invoke *force majeure* in the sense of emergency if:

- they have carefully weighed the relevant duties and interests at stake;
- they have done so in accordance with medical ethics and according to the medical-professional standard; and
- in doing so, and given the case's particular circumstances, they have made a choice that can be justified objectively.[21]

It also listed several factors that may be important in the assessment:

- whether, according to professional medical judgment, it was to be feared the person would suffer increasingly from loss of dignity or that their suffering, already experienced as unbearable, would worsen;
- whether it was foreseeable that the person would soon be unable to die with dignity;
- whether there were still possibilities to alleviate the suffering.[22]

It is tempting to associate the first two factors with the principle of respect for autonomy. Yet that would amount to an incorrect reading of the ruling. The Supreme Court did not discuss patient self-determination. It considered the factors mentioned primarily as elements of suffering. The Supreme Court overturned the appellate court's judgment and referred the case to the The Hague Court of Appeal, which upheld the appeal to *force majeure* and dismissed the charges against Dr. Schoonheim.[23]

A considerable period elapsed between the judgment of the Court of Appeal and that of the Supreme Court. More than likely, the decision had been postponed to take note of the position of the Royal Dutch Medical Association (KNMG).[24] That physicians' organization is another major contributor to Dutch euthanasia policy.

1.2.4 The Royal Dutch Medical Association

Euthanasia was on the agenda of the Association's general assembly meeting a week before the Supreme Court's ruling in the Schoonheim case. Its board had previously published its position on euthanasia in the Association's weekly magazine. The board had accepted that euthanasia was now practiced in medicine in the Netherlands, and it was also convinced that doctors were the only ones who should be allowed to perform euthanasia.[25]

The KNMG board wished to remove the legal uncertainty among physicians who may be considering performing euthanasia by formulating due care requirements. For the physician's action to be responsible, the patient's request had to be well-considered and based on their free will. The desire to die had to be sustained and the suffering unacceptable. In addition, the physician who was asked to perform euthanasia had to consult an experienced colleague. Finally, the board considered it fundamentally wrong to register a case of euthanasia as a natural death. The board not only argued that not filling out death certificates truthfully is unworthy of a medical professional, but it also felt that everything that takes place in medicine under the heading of euthanasia should be verifiable. In addition, the board was aware that obfuscating the cause of death in cases of euthanasia would only add to the existing tension between the law and medical practice.[26]

Dutch courts have always been clear about falsifying death certificates. The obligation to report unnatural deaths is strict. In the Rademaker case (1987), the Supreme Court ruled that euthanasia should always be regarded as a nonnatural cause of death, even if death is inevitable and the moment of dying naturally very near.[27]

At the assembly, the Association's President concluded the item by reiterating the board's explicit wish not to take a moral position on euthanasia. The intention was merely to offer guidance to individual members of the profession contemplating the performance of euthanasia.[28]

1.2.5 Chabot (1994)

The fact that the Dutch courts chose to be guided by the views of the medical profession was also evident in another case, involving a fifty-year-old woman who had ended her life by taking lethal drugs provided by her psychiatrist,

Dr. Chabot. For years, she had been suffering mentally because of past marital problems, the resulting divorce, and the death of both her young sons. After these events, and notwithstanding years of counseling, the woman was determined to die. Dr. Chabot found his patient to suffer continuously, unbearably, and hopelessly. Although she was physically healthy and her suffering was not the result of a psychiatric condition or disorder, there was a complicated grieving process with symptoms of depression. According to the psychiatrist, this condition was treatable, but the patient consistently rejected all further treatment. If she were not offered physician-assisted suicide, she would most likely try to commit suicide herself. The woman had previously saved up medication and attempted suicide. Everything indicated she could make another attempt. Following consultations in writing with seven experts (fellow psychiatrists and ethicists), Dr. Chabot agreed that the woman no longer had any realistic prospects for treatment.

The District Court and the Court of Appeal honored Dr. Chabot's appeal to *force majeure*.[29] However, the Supreme Court did not, and found the psychiatrist guilty without imposing a penalty.[30] Dr. Chabot was blamed primarily because none of the consulted experts had personally examined the patient. Therefore, the untreatability of the suffering had been insufficiently established. In particular, as the suffering was not somatic, the Court considered examination in person by a consultant to be essential.[31]

In addition, it also clarified the following points:

- Psychiatric patients can also request euthanasia voluntarily and well-considered.
- The cause of suffering does not affect the degree to which it is experienced. In other words, the hopelessness and unbearableness matter, not the cause (somatic, psychological, or other).
- Therefore, suffering caused by a psychiatric illness or disorder can justify euthanasia as well.
- In the event of such suffering, courts of law must assess the doctor's appeal to *force majeure* as an emergency with extra caution because (1) it must be ruled out that the illness or disorder influenced the patient's decision-making ability, and (2) it is more difficult to establish the unbearableness and the hopelessness of suffering stemming from a psychiatric cause.
- In principle, there can be no hopeless suffering if the patient freely refuses realistic alternatives for relief.[32]

1.2.6 Parliament and Government

The years 1984–1986 proved decisive for Dutch euthanasia policy. Although there was hardly any political input until that period, from 1980 onwards political parties began to make their views known. In 1984, the first bill was introduced, a private member's bill by social liberal MP Mrs. Elida Wessel-Tuinstra.[33] However, this bill met with resistance from the then center-right government.[34]

In 1989, the subsequent center-left government ordered an inquiry into the practice of euthanasia.[35] Since this study could not be conducted without the cooperation of physicians, some of their wishes were granted: a notification procedure for euthanasia and guidelines for its judicial handling.[36] Subsequently, the study revealed that in 1990 euthanasia had been performed an estimated 2,300 times, and assisted suicide about 400 times. It also revealed that a life was ended about 1,000 times without the patient's request. In only 40 percent of cases had a report been made of the decision-making process; and in only 18 percent of cases had the doctor reported an unnatural death.[37]

Parliament agreed to the government's proposal to provide the notification procedure developed for the purpose of the study with a legal basis.[38] This was implemented in June 1994. Until the enactment of the Euthanasia Act in 2002, the legal prohibition of euthanasia existed alongside a regulation as to the method of reporting cases – a typical example of Dutch pragmatism.

In 1994, a government without Christian Democrats took office, which had not been seen since 1918, and another study was conducted. As it turned out, the number of euthanasia cases had increased to 3,200 in 1995, but the number of physician-assisted suicide cases had remained the same. The number of times termination of life had occurred without the patient's explicit request had dropped to 900. The proportion of cases in which peer consultation had taken place had increased to 92 percent, and the notification percentage had risen to 41 percent.[39] Because this percentage was considered too low, the government proposed that regional euthanasia review committees be placed between the notifying physicians and the Public Prosecutor's Office. These would have to assess whether a doctor reporting a case of euthanasia or assisted suicide had acted in accordance with the due care requirements. And if that were the case, the committee should advise not to prosecute.[40]

In 1998, the government introduced a bill.[41] The Act on the Assessment of Termination of Life on Request and Assistance in Suicide (the "Euthanasia Act") came into force on April 1, 2002. This Act formalized the notification procedure and the consultation requirement while strengthening the review committees' position. Since the Euthanasia Act came into force, they no longer have a purely advisory role. If a review committee rules that a notifying doctor has met the due care requirements, it does not inform the Public Prosecutor's Office (and the Healthcare Inspectorate) of the facts.[42] The case is then closed.

The Act added nothing to the due care requirements. But for a proper understanding of these requirements, we have one last court ruling to consider.

1.2.7 Brongersma (2002)

In April 1998, former senator Edward Brongersma ended his life by taking lethal drugs given to him by his family doctor. Eighty-six-year-old Mr. Brongersma had no severe physical illnesses, nor any psychiatric disease or disorder, apart from some age-related complaints such as dizziness and osteoporosis. However, he suffered tremendously from his deterioration, loneliness, dependence on others, and a great sense of futility. Mr. Brongersma also feared that if he delayed too long, he would no longer be physically able to commit his desired suicide.

His general practitioner, Dr. Sutorius, had many conversations with his patient, and he concluded that his wish to die was durable, well-considered, and had come about voluntarily. The doctor was empathetic to Brongersma's suffering. After consulting a psychiatrist and ruling out a psychiatric disorder, he concluded that no more treatment options were available. A fellow general practitioner and a psychiatrist confirmed the unbearableness and hopelessness of the patient's suffering. Thereupon, Dr. Sutorius assisted in Mr. Brongersma's suicide.

The District Court considered that there was no consensus in medical ethics as to whether a narrow or a broad definition should be used regarding the unbearableness of suffering. The judges opted for a broad one. Because all the due care requirements had been met, the physician could, according to the District Court, rightly invoke *force majeure* and the charges against him were subsequently dropped.[43]

The Public Prosecutor's Office questioned whether being "tired of life," being "done with living," or "suffering from life" fell within the medical domain. According to the prosecution, the due care requirements developed in case law and those of the forthcoming Euthanasia Act were limited to that domain. The Court of Appeal endorsed this view and found the general practitioner guilty but did not impose any penalty.[44] Dr. Sutorius appealed the Court's judgment in cassation. In December 2002, the Supreme Court decided that only suffering predominantly caused by a medically classifiable somatic or psychological illness or disorder can legitimize deliberate life-terminating acts by a physician. And in the case of Mr. Brongersma, it concluded, no such legitimization existed. Thus it revoked a core consideration of the Chabot judgment, according to which the cause of suffering is irrelevant.[45]

In its judgment, the Supreme Court referred extensively to the legislative history of the Euthanasia Act. And because it was rendered after the latter's enactment, the so-called classification requirement is inextricably linked to the Act's criterion of suffering.

1.3 Why in the Netherlands?

Why, precisely, it was in the Netherlands that euthanasia was eventually legalized (or partly decriminalized) and not, or only much later, elsewhere, is a question many have pondered. American-Dutch historian James Kennedy listed some of the explanations given.[46] First, everyone in the Netherlands is mandatorily insured against medical expenses. In such a healthcare system, euthanasia can be practiced without the fear of financial motives or lack of care influencing the decision to terminate life intentionally. Such reasons are, of course, morally unacceptable. But similar healthcare systems exist in other countries as well, in those where the legalization of euthanasia has never been considered seriously.[47]

Second, the unique position of the Dutch general practitioner or family doctor was put forward by Kennedy. General practitioners are responsible for the majority of euthanasia cases. These doctors maintain close relationships with their patients. They live nearby, have usually known their patients for years, visit them at their homes, and are characterized by considerable emotional involvement. General practitioners can sympathize with patients requesting euthanasia. It has been suggested that geriatricians and other specialists are more reticent because they are less likely to stop considering alternatives and usually work as part of a team in settings (nursing homes and hospitals) less suited to euthanasia; other team members may feel differently about euthanasia, and institutions always have policies to which employees must adhere.[48]

Kennedy also pointed to the headroom for self-regulation given to the Dutch medical profession. The Public Prosecutor's Office operates on the basis of expediency. Very often, no trial was brought in cases of euthanasia, and where prosecution did occur, the courts appeared willing to be guided by the profession's views. Euthanasia has, therefore, always remained a question for the profession: Is it morally acceptable as medical practice? If it had presented itself as a patients' rights or a civil rights issue, the acceptance of euthanasia in the Netherlands would almost certainly have taken more time.[49]

Finally, Kennedy presented a cultural explanation for the euthanasia policy, one that has been given by many. The Netherlands has a strong tradition of pragmatism. Administratively, pragmatism is shown in attempts to control practices by regulating them, so they do not continue underground and evade supervision. Proponents of the Dutch euthanasia policy often refer to it as realistic because it attempts to control a practice that would exist regardless.[50] Pragmatism can also be seen as a corollary of Dutch consensus politics. In the Dutch political system, parliament and government rarely take the lead. The hallmark of this system is a deep-rooted desire to avoid conflict. The manner in which parliament and government have dealt with the euthanasia issue is a prime example. By postponing decisions, setting up advisory bodies, and repeatedly ordering studies, politicians have sought to avoid conflict. However, by constantly depoliticizing the issue in this way, other societal parties were able to resolve the issue. Only when all the building blocks of the euthanasia policy had been brought forward and put in place by others did politicians succeed in turning a bill into law.

As a pragmatic response to a social development, the Dutch euthanasia policy is not known for its clear principles.[51] It is a compromise offering something for everyone: euthanasia is prohibited by law, but the law makes exceptions; there is some recognition of patient self-determination, but the decision to grant euthanasia is reserved to the doctor. Therefore, the policy can be viewed in very different ways. It is correct to label the Dutch euthanasia policy as liberal and progressive, but the qualification "conservative" is equally appropriate. The policy is emancipatory and, at the same time, very paternalistic. It is both flexible and rigid. And because it is all of these things, because of its inconsistencies, it is also continuously being challenged.

1.4 The Euthanasia Act

The introduction of the Euthanasia Act resulted in amendments to the Criminal Code and the Burial and Cremation Act. The due care requirements were included in a separate law, the Euthanasia Act itself. The revision of the Criminal Code was limited to what properly belongs in that Code: the provisions prohibiting termination of life on request and assistance in suicide together with the ground for impunity.

The amendment of the Burial and Cremation Act was intended to ensure that, after being reported to the municipal coroner, cases of termination of life on request and assistance in suicide are sent for review to the regional euthanasia review committees. Their mission, composition, and competences are again found in the Euthanasia Act.

1.4.1 Criminal Code

Since April 1, 2002, the provisions of the Criminal Code read as follows. The italicized parts are the additions due to the Euthanasia Act.

Article 293 Criminal Code

1. A person who intentionally terminates the life of another at their express and earnest desire shall be punished by imprisonment for a term not exceeding twelve years or a fifth category fine.

2. *The fact referred to in the first paragraph is not punishable if it is committed by a physician who thereby complies with the requirements of care referred to in Article 2 of the Act on the Assessment of Termination of Life on Request and Assistance in Suicide and notifies the municipal coroner following Article 7, paragraph 2 of the Burial and Cremation Act.*

Article 294 Criminal Code

1. A person who intentionally incites another to commit suicide shall, if the suicide follows, be punished by imprisonment for a term not exceeding three years or a fourth category fine.

2. A person who intentionally assists another in suicide or provides them with the means to do so shall, if the suicide follows, be punished with imprisonment for a term not exceeding three years or a fine of the fourth category. *Article 293, paragraph 2, applies mutatis mutandis.*

1.4.2 Due Care Criteria, Written Requests, and Minors

The due care requirements are formulated in Article 2, paragraph 1 of the Euthanasia Act as follows:

1. To comply with the due care criteria referred to in Article 293, paragraph 2 of the Criminal Code, the physician must:

   a. be satisfied that the patient's request is voluntary and well-considered;
   b. be satisfied that the patient's suffering is unbearable, with no prospect of improvement;
   c. have informed the patient about their situation and prognosis;
   d. have concluded, together with the patient, that there is no reasonable alternative in the patient's situation;
   e. have consulted at least one other, independent physician, who must see the patient and give a written opinion on whether the due care criteria set out in (a) to (d) have been fulfilled;
   f. have exercised due medical care and attention in terminating the patient's life or assisting in suicide.

Paragraphs 2, 3, and 4 of Article 2 of the Euthanasia Act contain the following provisions regarding written advance directives requesting euthanasia and minors:

2. If a patient aged sixteen or over who is no longer capable of expressing their will but before reaching this state was deemed capable of making a reasonable appraisal of their interests, has made a written declaration requesting that their life be terminated, the physician may comply with their request. The due care criteria in paragraph 1 apply mutatis mutandis.

3. If the patient is a minor aged between sixteen and eighteen and is deemed to be capable of making a reasonable appraisal of their interests, the physician may comply with a request made by the patient to terminate their life or provide suicide assistance, after the parent or parents who have responsibility for him, or else their guardian, has or have been consulted.
4. If the patient is a minor aged between twelve and sixteen and is deemed to be capable of making a reasonable appraisal of their interests, the physician may, if a parent or the parents who have responsibility for him, or else their guardian, can agree to the termination of life or assisted suicide, comply with the patient's request. Paragraph 2 applies mutatis mutandis.

1.4.3 Notification Procedure

Notification and review were considered indispensable by the legislator. On the one hand, the procedure ensures proper monitoring and continuous improvement of the quality of life-terminating acts on request by physicians; on the other, it ensures that the practice of euthanasia is transparent and verifiable.[52]

Since the Euthanasia Act came into force, the notification procedure for the termination of life on request and the provision of assisted suicide is as follows. In accordance with the requirements of the Burial and Cremation Act, the doctor does not prepare a death certificate but reports an unnatural death to the municipal coroner and provides them with a reasoned account.[53] The coroner, in turn, notifies the Registrar's Office and the Public Prosecutor's Office to obtain a certificate of no objection to burial or cremation.[54] The municipal coroner verifies how and by what means the patient's life was ended;[55] they then forward the doctor's report to the competent regional euthanasia review committee.[56]

1.4.4 The Regional Euthanasia Review Committee

There are five regional euthanasia review committees composed of a lawyer acting as chairperson, a physician, and an ethicist. They assess whether the physician acted in accordance with the statutory due care requirements. The committee rules within six weeks of receiving the report and its ruling is communicated to the physician in writing. The case is closed if the committee rules that the doctor has acted with due care. If, in the committee's opinion, the doctor did not meet the statutory requirements, its findings are sent to the Board of Procurators General of the Public Prosecutor's Office and the Healthcare Inspectorate. Each of these parties will decide whether action should be taken, and if so, what form the action should take.[57]

The regional euthanasia review committees assess reported cases of euthanasia against the statutory due care requirements and, in doing so, they interpret them. Some years ago, the euthanasia review committees laid down their policy in a guideline. The *Euthanasia Code 2018* (revised in 2020 and 2022) outlines the aspects and considerations that the committees consider relevant regarding the statutory due care requirements. The *Code* can be found on the committees' website. It should be seen as a summary of the considerations published by the committees, of particular interest to physicians and consultants as well as meeting the information needs of patients who wish to make a request for euthanasia and of other interested parties.

1.5 "Euthanasia"

Finally, a few remarks on the meaning and use of the term "euthanasia." Etymologically, it simply means "good death." But to what practices does it refer? The official title of the Euthanasia Act accurately reflects the meaning of "euthanasia." It relates to two acts deemed criminal in the Netherlands: termination of life on request and assisting in suicide. *Sensu lato*, euthanasia means both; *sensu stricto*, it is the termination of life on request. The sense in which it is used, including in this Element, should be apparent from the context. Only when it is used in conjunction with "assisting in suicide" (or "assisted suicide"), does it have the narrow meaning.

Sensu lato, "euthanasia" refers to two criminal acts. Legally, perpetrators enjoy impunity if they: (1) are physicians; (2) have acted in accordance with the statutory due care requirements; and (3) have reported their actions in accordance with the procedure prescribed by law. Euthanasia in this sense is considered nonstandard medical practice in the Netherlands, partly because – unlike standard medical practice – it is embedded in criminal law. Euthanasia in this sense must be distinguished from acts resulting from medical decisions concerning the end of life, which are seen in the Netherlands as standard medicine. Discontinuing or not initiating a life-saving or life-extending medical procedure at the request of a patient or their representative(s) is not euthanasia. Neither is euthanasia the failure to perform (or discontinue) a medically futile procedure. Even when this is done without the consent of the patient or their representative(s), it is still not euthanasia. In the Netherlands, the procedure known as palliative or terminal sedation (administering drugs to keep the patient deeply sedated until death without giving artificial nutrition or hydration) is also considered standard medical practice. The same applies to pain relief with a (foreseeable) fatal side effect. The Euthanasia Act does not apply to these practices.

2 Trends in Dutch Euthanasia Practice

The Regional Euthanasia Review Committees are legally bound to publish annual reports.[58] By also publishing anonymized rulings, the review committees try to provide as much openness as possible about their assessment of cases against the statutory due care criteria. The annual reports and the rulings are posted on the website of the joint euthanasia review committees.[59]

In addition, the government is legally bound to commission independent, in-depth research into the functioning of the Euthanasia Act once every five years. Its results are sent to parliament and annexed to a governmental position paper. These studies are also valuable sources of information.

2.1 Some Numbers

According to the latest annual report, the committees received 8,720 notifications of euthanasia in 2022, that is, 5.1 percent of the total number of people who died in the Netherlands that year (169,938).[60] In 2003, the first full calendar year following the enactment, the euthanasia review committees received 1,815 notifications.[61]

The male/female ratio has not changed significantly over the years. In 2022, the numbers of male and female patients were 4,412 men (50.6 percent) and 4,308 women (49.4 percent).[62]

In 2022, there were 8,501 notifications of termination of life on request (97.4 percent of the total number of euthanasia notifications), 186 (2.1 percent) notifications of assisted suicide, and 33 notifications (0.38 percent) involving a combination of the two.[63] Such a combination occurs if, in cases of assisted suicide, the patient ingests the potion handed to them but does not die within the time agreed upon by the physician and the patient. The doctor then proceeds to terminate the patient's life by intravenously administering a coma-inducing substance, followed by a muscle relaxant. The termination of life on request/ assisted suicide ratio has remained constant.

As regards the most common conditions, 88.6 percent (7,726) of the notifications in 2022 involved patients with incurable cancer (5,046, 57.8 percent), neurological disorders (615, 7 percent), cardiovascular disease (359, 4.1 percent), pulmonary disorders (277, 3.2 percent) or a combination of conditions (1,429, 16.4 percent).[64] According to the 2004 annual report, the first one to list the most common conditions, 96 percent of notifications involved patients with incurable cancer.[65] Over the years, this percentage has been decreasing steadily.

Six notifications in 2022 involved patients in advanced stages of dementia who could no longer communicate their requests. In these cases, the advance directive was decisive in establishing whether the request was voluntary and well-considered. In 282 cases, the patient's suffering was caused by early-stage dementia. These patients were deemed competent regarding their request for euthanasia because they could still grasp its implications.[66] Over the years, the number of notifications involving patients with dementia has been increasing steadily. Performing euthanasia on patients in advanced stages of dementia is rare because of its difficulties, as we shall see in Section 3.1.

In 115 cases of euthanasia reported in 2022, the patient's suffering was caused by one or more psychiatric disorders.[67] The number of notifications involving patients with psychiatric disorders has almost doubled since 2018 (67).[68]

Multiple geriatric syndromes – such as sight impairment, hearing impairment, osteoporosis, osteoarthritis, and so on – may cause unbearable suffering without the prospect of improvement. These syndromes, often degenerative in nature, generally occur in elderly patients and are the sum of one or more disorders and related symptoms. In 2022, the review committees received 379 notifications of euthanasia (4.3 percent) that fell into this category.[69] These notifications have been increasing sharply in recent years, with 217 notifications in 2019, 235 in 2020, and 307 in 2021 (see Section 5).[70]

Lastly, the review committees register notifications involving conditions not falling into any of the above categories, such as chronic pain syndrome or rare genetic disorders, as "other conditions." There were 212 such cases in 2022.[71]

As far as age is concerned, the highest number of notifications of euthanasia involved patients in their seventies (2,873 cases, 32.9 percent), followed by patients in their eighties (2,314 cases, 26.5 percent) and people in their sixties (1,669 cases, 19.1 percent). In 2022, one notification of euthanasia involving a minor aged between twelve and seventeen was reviewed.[72] As regards age, no significant changes have occurred over the years.

In the vast majority of cases reported in 2022, as in previous years, the patient died at home (6,939 cases, 79.6 percent). Patients also died in hospices (667 cases, 7.7 percent), nursing homes (829 cases, 9.5 percent), hospitals (157 cases, 1.8 percent), or elsewhere, for instance, at the home of a family member or in a convalescent home (128 cases, 1.5 percent).[73] In 2022, most cases (7,013) were notified by a general practitioner (80.4 percent of the total number).[74]

In 2022, euthanasia was performed on two partners simultaneously, according to fifty-eight notifications (twenty-nine couples, a record).[75] According to the revised *Euthanasia Code 2018*, both partners must be seen by different independent physicians to ensure an independent consultation.[76] Since 2018, the number of notifications involving couples has been mentioned in the annual reports (twenty-six in 2020, thirty-six in 2019, eighteen in 2018, and thirty-two in 2021).[77]

And finally, in thirteen of the notified cases in 2022 (0.15 percent of all notifications), the Euthanasia Review Committees found that the notifying physician had not complied with all the due care requirements set out in the Euthanasia Act.[78] Since its enactment, similar numbers have been reported annually. As required by law, these notifications were all forwarded to the Public Prosecutor's Office and the Healthcare Inspectorate. In all cases except one, the former decided not to prosecute. The rulings in the Arends case (better known as the Coffee Euthanasia case) is discussed in Section 3.1.

2.2 Supplementary Information

The Euthanasia Act is meant to provide legal certainty for all involved, to assure prudent practice with regard to euthanasia by physicians, and to provide an adequate framework for physicians to be accountable and for increased transparency and societal control. Its functioning is evaluated by independent academics once every five years. Since its enactment, four evaluation studies have taken place.

The latest evaluation study focused on the practice of end-of-life decisions, developments in the conceptualization and interpretation of the legal requirements, and potential problems and complexities of the review system in 2017–2022.[79] The findings supplement the information in the euthanasia review committees' annual reports.

The picture that emerged from 2017–2022 was similar to that in previous periods. On the issue of legal certainty, the evaluation study found that 82 percent of Dutch doctors are willing to perform euthanasia or provide assisted suicide under the current rules. And, almost always, the statutory due care criteria are met.[80] Each year, the committees ruled in only a few cases that the physician had not fully complied with the statutory due care requirements. In most of these cases, the problem did not concern the so-called material requirements (the request, the suffering, the availability of reasonable alternatives) but the criteria regarding consultation and the medically prudent administration of euthanatics. Those rulings were subsequently forwarded to the Public Prosecutor's Office and the Healthcare Inspectorate. In only one case did the former initiate criminal proceedings (see Section 3.1).[81]

Second, notification is essential to achieve a transparent and controlled practice of euthanasia and physician-assisted suicide. In 2021, 83 percent of all estimated cases were reported to the Regional Euthanasia Review Committees, a percentage corresponding with the rates found in previous studies.[82] Failure to notify was found to be related to the fact that physicians do not qualify all cases as euthanasia. Apparently, these cases fall into a gray area; for instance, when using morphine as a drug to end life, it is often not possible to be certain that there has indeed been a life-shortening effect.[83]

Third, physicians who reported a case of euthanasia or assisted suicide generally experience the procedures of reporting and reviewing as neutral or positive.[84] The regional euthanasia review committees were found to function well.[85]

Fourth, the study showed that the general public supports the current regulation of ending life on request. The public's knowledge of the law is regarded as generally good, although there are misunderstandings concerning specific details.[86] Some believe the Act grants patients an enforceable legal right to euthanasia, as became evident in the Coffee Euthanasia case (see Section 3.1).[87]

And finally, the number of notified cases has been increasing steadily, from 1,815 in 2003 to 8,720 in 2022. Although it was recommended that the government commission research into the underlying causes in the previous evaluation study,[88] no explanation is given in the latest study. However, it is suggested that – because of a trend toward increasing periods of time people might have left to live – the demand for euthanasia is rising, including by those not yet in the very final stages of life.[89]

3 Euthanasia for the Incompetent

The Dutch Euthanasia Act is based on compassion. Although termination of life on request and assisting in suicide are far from being accepted as acts of compassion universally, Dutch criminal courts have at least been willing to grant impunity to physicians who have committed those offenses on the ground of *force majeure* in the sense of emergency. The courts have accepted as emergency a conflict of duties: a physician's duty to preserve life, on the one hand, and their duty to alleviate suffering, on the other. Doctors who have felt compelled to opt for the latter at the expense of their patient's life will not be punished, provided that certain conditions are met. And since the patient's voluntary and well-considered request is merely one of several necessary conditions, it is fair to say that the Euthanasia Act is ultimately not based on the principle of individual self-determination. The extent to which compassion is the driving force in Dutch euthanasia policymaking is often underestimated.

3.1 Incompetent, but Once Competent

Since the Brongersma ruling, no euthanasia cases had been brought before the Supreme Court of the Netherlands. Still, on April 21, 2020, it issued its judgments in what has become known as the Coffee Euthanasia case: the deliberate termination, in 2016, of the life of a seventy-four-year-old severely demented woman by a geriatrician in a nursing home in The Hague.[90] On that date, a four-year legal battle came to an end. No fewer than five adjudicating bodies ruled in this case. Each ruling made headlines and boosted public debate.

3.1.1 The Euthanasia Review Committee

The competent euthanasia review committee had ruled that the geriatrician – Dr. Arends – had not complied with the due care requirements.[91] To begin with, she could not have concluded unequivocally that the request was voluntary and well-considered. Her patient, who had Alzheimer's disease, had never made a verbal request for euthanasia, nor was there a clear, written advance directive to that effect.[92]

Considering the patient's history and the oral testimony given by the geriatrician and the patient's general practitioner, the committee established the patient was no longer competent when her life was ended, at least not insofar as regards euthanasia. She had never discussed this subject with the geriatrician, nor could she have discussed it. By her own admission, the geriatrician decided to terminate her patient's life solely on the basis of the patient's written advance directive.[93]

According to the review committees' policies at the time, which set out the practicalities of the statutory due care criteria, a written advance directive must make clear that it is unmistakably applicable to the situation that has arisen. The physician must then consider the patient's medical history and all the other specific circumstances. They must interpret the patient's behavior and statements, both during the course of the illness and immediately preceding the performance of the euthanasia. At that moment, it must be abundantly clear that performing euthanasia is commensurate with the advance directive and that there are no contraindications (i.e. clear signs that the patient does not want to have their life terminated). At that moment, it will also have to be clear that the patient experiences their suffering as unbearable.[94]

In this case, shortly after being diagnosed with Alzheimer's, and four years before her death, the patient had drawn up a written advance directive with a dementia clause. Her reasons for wanting euthanasia were apparent: she did not want to go into a nursing home for elderly people with dementia, and she wanted to part with her nearest and dearest in a dignified manner before it would be too late.[95] Originally, the dementia clause began with: "I want to exercise my legal right to have voluntary euthanasia performed on me *when I am still somewhat competent and when I am no longer able to live at home with my husband*" (emphasis added).[96]

However, it became apparent that the patient had changed her advance directive one year before she died. The first sentence now read: "I want to exercise my legal right to have euthanasia performed on me *when I consider the time right for such*" (emphasis added).[97] And whereas in the earlier version of the directive the clause had ended with "Trusting that by the time the quality of my life has reached the situation described above, I be euthanized voluntarily,"[98] in the second version, the last sentence now read as follows: "Trusting that at such time as the quality of my life has become so poor *that euthanasia be performed at my request.*"[99]

In the year before her death, the patient had made it clear to her general practitioner that she did not want to go into a nursing home and that, if this were to happen, she wanted euthanasia to be performed. According to her general practitioner, the patient had never expressed a desire for euthanasia to be performed when she was still competent. And although, by the end of the year, she had apparently frequently said at home that she wanted to die (but always with the addition "but not now"), she had never actually asked the general practitioner to perform euthanasia. The review committee considered it plausible that the woman had lost her competence to decide on euthanasia during that year. When she was eventually admitted to a nursing home, her husband asked the resident geriatrician to perform euthanasia on the basis of her written advance directive.[100]

The review committee found there were two mutually exclusive dementia clauses, resulting in doubts about whether the patient wanted the written advance directive to replace a verbal request. Taking also into account the irreversibility of termination of life, the committee concluded that the physician should have erred on the side of caution. It therefore considered that the provisions in the Euthanasia Act concerning a written advance directive were not applicable in this case. And, because a verbal request had also not been made, the review committee concluded the geriatrician had not complied with the first statutory due care requirement.[101]

As regards the requirement of due medical care and attention in terminating the patient's life, the committee concluded as follows. Prior to the euthanasia, the geriatrician had put Dormicum (midazolam) in her patient's coffee. This had been done surreptitiously, although it had been discussed with the patient's husband and daughter, to deprive her of the opportunity to resist the administration of the lethal drug. Furthermore, when the drip was inserted, the patient shied away. She woke up and tried to sit up when the thiopental was being administered.[102] Her family helped hold her down so the geriatrician could quickly administer the remainder of the dose. According to the review committee, the physician wrongfully failed to consider whether this could be interpreted as a relevant sign that the patient did not want the drip inserted or injected with a syringe. Indeed, she should have seriously considered this possibility. Therefore, the physician should have ceased the procedure to assess the situation, and she should not have continued once the patient had to be held down. The committee emphasized that coercion, or even the appearance of coercion, needs to be avoided at all times.[103]

3.1.2 Disciplinary Boards and District Court

The committee's ruling was subsequently forwarded to the Public Prosecutor's Office and the Healthcare Inspectorate. Both decided to act. Initially, the latter met with success. The Regional Disciplinary Board for Healthcare ruled that the Inspectorate's complaint was well-founded and reprimanded the geriatrician.[104] On appeal, the Central Disciplinary Board for Healthcare reduced the sanction to a warning. It found that the physician had acted reprehensibly, but only "to a limited extent." The Board's lowering of the sanction was primarily motivated by the thoroughness of the physician's examinations before her patient's death and the degree to which other healthcare professionals were involved. She had also sought advice from several other professional care providers. And, unlike the Regional Disciplinary Board, the Central Disciplinary Board sympathized with the manner in which the geriatrician had administered the Dormicum.[105]

After the Central Disciplinary Board had ruled, the District Court rendered its judgment in the criminal case. The Public Prosecutor's Office had principally charged the physician with performing termination of life on request and, alternatively, with murder. But it had also asked the District Court not to impose a penalty.[106] The District Court considered there to be sufficient proof for an express and earnest desire on the part of the patient, as required by Article 293, paragraph 1 of the Criminal Code. According to the Court, it was apparent from discussions in parliament at the time that the legislator clearly intended termination of life on the basis of an advance directive to fall within the scope of the Euthanasia Act. And in this case, an advance directive was at hand. Perhaps the dementia clause was not entirely unambiguous. Still, if it were to be interpreted that the patient only wanted euthanasia as long as she could decide the exact moment herself, this would have deprived her advance directive of any meaning.[107]

According to the Public Prosecutor's Office, it was apparent from the parliamentary proceedings that the first due care requirement entails an obligation to verify written advance directives so long as incompetent patients can still make concrete and coherent statements about whether they want to live or die. The geriatrician had failed to comply with this requirement.[108] The District Court considered obtaining verbal verification from an incompetent patient about their wishes or suffering to be impossible. Such a requirement would obviate an advance directive. The Court was aware of the existence of medical guidelines which also oblige physicians to try to verify the current viewpoints of patients regarding ending life in the event of incompetence; however, in its opinion, these rules were stricter than the statutory requirements. Legally, according to the District Court, such an obligation does not exist.[109]

The defendant and the Public Prosecutor's Office subsequently agreed to bring the criminal case immediately before the highest judicial body in the Netherlands. In addition, the Procurator General lodged an appeal in cassation against the decision of the Central Disciplinary Board, something that had never occurred before.

3.1.3 The Supreme Court and the Euthanasia Code Revised

On April 21, 2020, the Supreme Court pronounced two judgments.[110] In the criminal case, it upheld the ruling of the District Court. By dismissing the charges against the geriatrician, the District Court had not erred; the geriatrician had acted with appropriate due care.

According to the Supreme Court, the Euthanasia Act is unambiguous: a physician is allowed to act based on a written request for termination of life once that has been made by a patient. For a physician to be allowed to carry out such a request, the Act stipulates that the patient must be no longer capable of expressing their will. It does not make any distinction with respect to the possible causes of that incapacity. However, it is apparent from the parliamentary proceedings that the legislator explicitly included dementia as such a possible cause. A physician, therefore, has an obligation to interpret a written request to determine the patient's intentions. In doing so, they must consider all the relevant circumstances and not just the literal wording of the request. At a minimum, the request must be such that the patient asks for termination of life in a situation where they can no longer determine or express their will about having their life ended due to advanced dementia. Moreover, if the patient wants to see this request carried out in cases where there is no physical unbearable suffering, it will have to be clear from the request that the patient considers their (future) state of advanced dementia itself to be unbearable. Furthermore, it is essential that the physician carefully assesses the patient's current situation so as to compare this situation with the circumstances described in the written request, whereby the physician has to pay special attention to contraindications conflicting with that request in the period following the drafting of the request by the patient, in particular oral statements by the patient inconsistent with that request. If these statements are made in the period after the point at which the patient is no longer able to determine or express their own will due to advanced dementia, they can no longer be automatically construed as an expression of will explicitly aimed at the withdrawal or modification of the earlier written request.[111]

The Supreme Court also quashed the decision of the Central Disciplinary Board in the disciplinary case. Its view that – in principle – there is no room for interpretation of a written request, was considered incorrect.[112]

Because of both rulings, the joint euthanasia review committees felt compelled to amend the *Euthanasia Code 2018*, which sets out their interpretation of the statutory due care requirements. Consequently, the *Code* provides guidance for physicians considering requests for euthanasia, too. The following changes were made:

1. The written advance directive containing a request for termination of life must be interpreted with a view to ascertaining the patient's intention. In doing so, the physician must consider all the circumstances of the case and not merely the literal wording of the written request. Thus, there is room for interpretation.
2. Determining whether there is hopeless and unbearable suffering in the case of advanced dementia is a medical-professional judgment reserved for the physician. Therefore, the euthanasia review committee must exercise restraint in evaluating this professional medical judgment and ask whether the doctor could reasonably conclude that the patient was suffering unbearably.
3. When euthanasia is to be performed on a patient who is incompetent as a result of advanced dementia, the physician does not need to consult with the patient about the time and manner in which the euthanasia will be carried out. Such a conversation is futile because such a patient lacks understanding regarding this topic.
4. If there are indications that agitation or aggression may occur during the performance of euthanasia on an incompetent patient, the medical standards to be observed by the physician may lead them to conclude that premedication is appropriate.[113]

3.1.4 A Lost Opportunity

The Supreme Court only referred to the Act's legislative history in its rulings. There are no references to fundamental rights, which is remarkable, even incomprehensible. One can only speculate why it decided to limit applicable law in this way. Of course, judicial review of statute law against fundamental rights as protected by the Dutch Constitution is not an issue since the latter prohibits this. Still, treaty provisions such as those of the Convention for the Protection of Human Rights and Fundamental Freedoms (or the European Convention on Human Rights, ECHR), to which the Netherlands is a party, are justiciable. The Constitution requires national courts of law to declare laws of national origin inapplicable if they are incompatible with self-executing international treaty provisions.[114]

The Dutch Euthanasia Act is believed to be generally consistent with relevant ECHR provisions,[115] as the European Court of Human Rights (ECtHR) in Strasbourg has adopted a wide margin of appreciation in its rulings on assisted suicide. However, the Coffee Euthanasia case was obviously a hard case. On several occasions, the ECtHR has ruled that decisions about one's death fall within the scope of ECHR, Article 8. In *Haas* v. *Switzerland* (2011), it stated: "an individual's right to decide by what means and at what point his or her life will end, provided he or she is capable, or of freely reaching a decision on this question and acting in consequence, is one of the aspects of the right to respect for private life within the meaning of Article 8 of the Convention."[116]

However, interferences with the exercise of this right are permitted. The ECtHR continued as follows:

> In consequence, it is appropriate to refer, in the context of examining a possible violation of Article 8, to Article 2 of the Convention, which creates for the authorities a duty to protect vulnerable persons, even against actions by which they endanger their own lives. . . . For the Court, this latter Article obliges national authorities to prevent an individual from taking his or her own life if the decision has not been taken freely and with a full understanding of what is involved.[117]

The Strasbourg Court has acknowledged that state parties to the ECHR have divergent views on voluntary termination of life; a positive state obligation to facilitate euthanasia or assisted suicide is therefore not implied in Article 8. But, when a state does decide to allow such practices, it is obligated – because of the right to life as protected by Article 2 – to implement measures to prevent those who are unable to make such a decision freely and with a full understanding of its implications from taking their own lives; measures that may restrict the exercise of everyone's right to decide by what means and at what point their own life will end.

The Supreme Court missed the opportunity to test the Euthanasia Act's provision on written euthanasia requests against Articles 2 and 8 of the ECHR. Therefore, we do not know whether it considers it within the margin adopted by the ECtHR. From a fundamental rights perspective, we are kept in the dark as to whether the incompetent but once competent are protected by the right to life or the right to respect for privacy. Constitutionally, the Supreme Court did not do what it is supposed to do. Its rulings in the Coffee Euthanasia case are authoritative merely because of their judicial ranking, not because of their merits.

Apparently, Article 2, paragraph 2 of the Dutch Euthanasia Act was in as much need of interpretation as the patient's written euthanasia request.[118] Interpreted literally, the Act's due care criteria require the patient to be fully competent at the time of euthanasia. Such a patient's will can easily be determined. However, once they are "no longer capable of expressing their will," or seem incapable of doing so, the written request for euthanasia that was drafted when they were "capable of making a reasonable appraisal of their interests" becomes guiding. According to the Supreme Court, the ability to express or determine one's will is something a demented patient can lose, and once it is lost – to be determined by the physician – it is lost forever. Whether that is consistent with the realities of dementia or not, something of a caesura is assumed between a former self and a present self, if there is such a thing as a present self in patients with advanced dementia.

A request for euthanasia by a former self somewhat resembles euthanasia asked for by a third party. Euthanasia requested by a proper third party is also possible in the Netherlands.

3.2 Severely Suffering Newborns

According to the Dutch Euthanasia Act, decisional competent patients aged twelve and over can request euthanasia. Intentionally and premeditated depriving another person of their life without their request constitutes murder according to Article 289 of the Dutch Criminal Code. This provision is supplemented by Article 82a of the Criminal Code, which states that "another person" also includes a child at or shortly after birth. Therefore, a physician who intentionally ends the life of a severely suffering minor under the age of twelve risks being convicted of murder, unless – again – that physician can successfully invoke *force majeure* in the sense of emergency.

3.2.1 The Groningen Protocol

On March 15, 2007, the Netherlands introduced rules on the intentional termination of life of newborns (children under the age of one) suffering severely. Those rules, revised on February 1, 2016 and laid down in a ministerial regulation, are by and large similar to the ones on euthanasia: they are embedded in criminal law, they require the fulfillment of due care requirements, and they provide for procedures of notification and review by an expert committee.

These rules are the result of developments in the 1990s. In 1992, the Dutch Pediatrics Association published a much-debated report on the limitations of neonatology.[119] And in the mid 1990s, the question of whether one could speak of due care and whether the physician in question could, therefore, successfully invoke *force majeure* in specific cases was also submitted to the court in two cases, those of Prins (1995) and Kadijk (1996).[120]

In March 1993, at the parents' request, Dr. Prins administered a lethal injection to a severely handicapped newborn who was in great pain and did not have long to live. The Court of Appeal granted the gynecologist impunity since he had acted with due care. And in April 1994, Dr. Kadijk ended the life of a severely handicapped three-week-old girl. The child suffered from a chromosomal abnormality, was in great pain, and had little chance of life. At the request of the parents, who wanted to take care of their firstborn and let her die at home, the doctor allowed the child to die peacefully in her mother's arms. In the Netherlands, treatment of a nonviable newborn infant is usually not initiated. In the Kadijk case, however, treatment was started. The baby was even resuscitated on the second day when a respiratory arrest occurred. But since the girl could not drink and needed to be tube fed, an emergency was created compelling the general practitioner to act. Dr. Kadijk was granted impunity by the appellate court.

Even though the charges against both physicians were dismissed, doctors felt burdened by the risk of being prosecuted for murder, despite being convinced of having acted responsibly. Partly in response to these concerns, the government decided, in 1996, to set up an advisory committee for termination of life in newborns, with the following task: "To advise on the basis of requirements of due care for medical intervention with respect to newborn infants with serious disorders, on a procedure for reporting and reviewing cases in which that intervention has led to deliberate termination of life."[121]

In its report, the committee considered that when it comes to decisions concerning the end of life in newborns, a distinction must be made between deliberate termination of life on the one hand and other decisions (such as refraining from treatment) on the other. While the latter are acts of standard medicine not requiring special review, decisions to hasten the end of life do require specific standards and specific review. The report then elaborated on the requirements of due care that are relevant in cases of intentional termination of life in severely ill newborns. In doing so, it followed the conditions formulated in the Prins and Kadijk court rulings. After considering the objectives of the assessment and the preconditions for adequate assessment, the committee expressed a preference for retrospective assessment by a national multidisciplinary review committee. It also felt that the existing criminal law framework should remain largely intact, due in part to the provisions of international law.[122]

Even before the government decided to set up a committee, the Dutch Pediatrics Association accepted a protocol for active termination of life in severely ill newborns as a national guideline in the spring of 2005. This protocol, better known as the Groningen Protocol as it was drawn up by the Groningen Academic Hospital, indicated how termination of life in severely ill newborns is to be handled with due care.[123] Although the protocol gave rise to international outcry,[124] it was consistent with the Prins and Kadijk court rulings as well as the advisory committee's recommendations. Later that year, the government decided to set up a national expert committee that would retrospectively assess against the required standards of care. To this end, the committee should receive information from the doctor via the municipal coroner. The committee's judgment would not replace the decision by the Public Prosecutor's Office as to whether to prosecute but – as an expert opinion – it would serve as advice. The committee would also review reported cases of late-term abortion, also a criminal offense according to Dutch law. The regulation came into effect in February 2007.[125]

3.2.2 Murder, Due Care, Notification, and Review

According to the Order establishing the Review Committee on Late-Term Abortions and Termination of Life in Newborns – as the regulation is called nowadays – and the accompanying instruction of the Public Prosecutor's Office, a physician is granted impunity if they successfully appeal to *force majeure* in the sense of emergency.[126]

A physician who has terminated a newborn's life is expected to notify the municipal coroner, who verifies how and by what means life was ended. The coroner must inform the Public Prosecutor's Office to obtain a certificate of no objection to burial or cremation and forward the doctor's report to the Review Committee on Late-Term Abortions and Termination of Life in Newborns.[127]

The Committee consists of six members. Its chair is appointed from among their number. Four members are physicians from several disciplines related to the issues at hand (gynecology, neonatology, and child neurology). One member is an expert in ethics, and one is a lawyer.[128] It reviews on the basis of due care criteria and communicates its findings to the physician and the Public Prosecutor's Office within six weeks. If the physician is found to have acted with due care, the latter will, in principle, not prosecute. If they are found not to have met the requirements, the Healthcare Inspectorate will also be informed.[129]

According to Article 7 of the Order, a physician has acted with due care in terminating the life of a neonate if:

1. that physician is convinced that the newborn suffers hopelessly and unbearably, which means, *i.a.,* that discontinuing medical treatment is justified, *i.e.* that, according to prevailing medical opinion, intervention is pointless and that, according to general medical opinion, there is no reasonable doubt about the diagnosis and the subsequent prognosis;

2. that physician has fully informed the parents of the diagnosis and the prognosis based on it and that the doctor has come to the conviction with the parents that for the situation in which the newborn found itself, there was no reasonable other solution;
3. the parents have consented to termination of life;
4. that physician has consulted at least one other independent physician who has given their opinion in writing regarding the abovementioned requirements of care or, if an independent physician could not reasonably be consulted, has consulted the medical team that has given its opinion in writing regarding the abovementioned requirements of due care;
5. the termination of life was carried out with due medical care.

The Review Committee publishes its findings on its website.[130] Since the predecessor of the current Order came into force in March 2007, it has received two notifications. In both cases, the physician was found to have acted with due care.[131]

The due care requirements of the Order differ significantly from those of the Euthanasia Act. First, the patients cannot request intentional life termination since they are incompetent. But whereas the Euthanasia Act stipulates that the patient requests and the physician consents, it is the parents who consent under the Order. As parental consent is the necessary condition, this implies that the physician can request to terminate their newborn's life. But it also allows parents to make a request themselves. When the Dutch health minister informed parliament in June 2022 of a forthcoming amendment to the Order (as discussed in the next paragraph), he had a letter accompanied by the results of a study into end-of-life decision-making concerning forty-four severely suffering children aged between one and twelve.[132] Brouwer, Maeckelberghe, and Verhagen presented ten cases in detail.[133] In all of these cases, the parents were the requesting party.[134] This implies that it is the parents who guide the physician regarding the unbearableness of the suffering, and this being its subjective aspect (as opposed to its hopelessness), since the child is unable to do so. Of course, this begs the question of whether the suffering of a severely ill child is really distinguishable from that of its parents.[135]

Second, although the Public Prosecutor's Office must always be informed, the actual number of notifications has been meager.[136] According to the latest evaluation study, published in 2022, this is probably due to low levels of confidence in the Review Committee and fear of criminal prosecution. Even when the Committee has determined that all requirements have been met, the Public Prosecutor's Office will still make its own assessment. When the occasion arises, doctors would rather opt for cessation of treatment rather than active termination of life.[137]

Finally, although the Review Committee has barely had the opportunity to interpret the due care requirements of the Order, because of the almost complete lack of notifications, it still saw fit to be more specific. Of particular interest is the definition given by the Review Committee in its annual reports of "termination of life in newborns," which is said to mean: "the deliberate shortening of a newborn infant's life where the child is suffering unbearably and is without prospect of improvement (current suffering) or can be expected to suffer unbearably and have no prospect of improvement in the future (future suffering). The child's state of health precludes any prospect of independent life."[138] This definition, which raises new questions, is not provided in the Order itself, nor can it be found in the explanatory memorandum provided by the responsible ministers.

3.3 Bridging the Gap

The Order establishing the Review Committee on Late-Term Abortions and Termination of Life in Newborns is a blatant concession to the desire of Dutch pediatricians and neonatologists to have termination of life in severely suffering newborn infants seen as an act of compassion. Since the Order only applies to children under the age of one, and since the Euthanasia Act is applicable from the age of 12, there are no rules for children with ages in between, apart from those of Articles 40 (on *force majeure*) and 289 (on murder) of the Criminal Code. It may not come as a surprise to learn that Dutch pediatricians and neonatologists have consistently been advocating specific rules for children in the 1–12 age range. And this has been successful, since new rules have recently been announced in parliament.

In 2019, the results were published of a four-year pediatric study on end-of-life care and decision-making.[139] According to the authors, there are no indications of active termination of life in children between the ages of one and twelve being practiced in the Netherlands. However, they noticed that for neonatologists and pediatricians a gray area exists between palliative sedation and active termination of life; for them, the boundaries between the two courses of action are unclear. In addition, those doctors knew of cases of unbearable and hopeless suffering in children, which they were not always able to alleviate sufficiently. Consequently, some doctors feel the need for clear rules on termination of life in cases of unbearable and hopeless suffering, in which no other reasonable solution exists.[140] In 2020, the health and justice ministers promised parliament they would provide rules specifically for active termination of life in children aged between one and twelve. A draft regulation was subsequently sent to parliament in June 2022.[141]

The draft proposes to amend the existing Order in just two ways. First, its (Dutch) name will be changed by adding "and Children," meaning children aged between one and twelve. And, second, an Article 7a will be inserted, which reads as follows:

> In the case of termination of a child's life, the physician has acted with due care if:
>
> a. that physician, on the basis of prevailing medical insight, could be convinced that the child's suffering was hopeless and unbearable;
> b. that physician was convinced that there was no reasonable possibility of removing the child's suffering, which means, among other things, that palliative care was or would have been insufficient to relieve the suffering;
> c. that physician fully informed the parents of the diagnosis and the prognosis based thereon, and that the physician discussed with the parents that termination of life was the only reasonable option to relieve the child's suffering;
> d. that physician discussed with the child, if capable of doing so, the diagnosis and the prognosis based thereon, in a manner appropriate to the child's comprehension, and the physician discussed with the child that termination of life was the only reasonable option to relieve suffering and there was no reasonable suspicion on the part of the physician that the termination of life was being carried out against the child's will;
> e. the parents have given their consent to termination of life being carried out;
> f. that physician has consulted at least one independent physician who has expertise relevant to the situation of the child and this physician has given their opinion in writing regarding the above-mentioned standards of care, or if giving a written opinion was not possible in a timely manner, has given their opinion orally and has subsequently recorded this oral opinion in writing, and
> g. the termination of life was carried out with due medical care.[142]

3.4 Preliminary Observations

In Dutch policymaking on euthanasia, a regulatory concept consisting of four components appears to be applied analogically. The rules on euthanasia are embedded in criminal law (1), they require the fulfillment of so-called due care requirements (2), and they provide for procedures of notification (3) and review by an expert committee (4). With each application, its content both changes and remains the same. Its structure remains intact with each application, but the components themselves are adjusted depending on the intended patient group.

In this section, three analogical applications of the regulatory concept have been discussed. Initially, the Euthanasia Act was clearly meant to cater to the needs of physicians facing requests for euthanasia by patients aged twelve and over who were deemed competent at the moment of euthanasia. However, the Euthanasia Act also applies to incompetent patients aged sixteen and over who have drafted an advance directive: the incompetent once competent. By simply stating that the Act's due care requirements apply *mutatis mutandis* in those cases,[143] the legislator left it to the euthanasia review committees to interpret them. However, their interpretation of the first requirement, subsequently adopted by both disciplinary boards, proved problematic. It had to be replaced by one provided by the Supreme Court.

In the second analogical application, the patient group being incompetent new-born infants up to the age of one, the other components were also adjusted. In addition to partly modified due care criteria, the criminal offense is no longer termination of life on request or suicide assistance but murder; the notification procedure is identical, but the review is done by another expert committee, one that will always inform the Public Prosecutor's Office. In the proposal for severely suffering children aged between one and twelve, the third application, those adjustments are adopted unchanged, but the due care requirements are modified once more.

It is safe to say that these analogical applications are, first and foremost, tailored to the needs of physicians contemplating euthanasia for incompetent patients.

3.4.1 The Need for Clarity and Comfort

Since 2012, the euthanasia review committees have registered cases of termination of life involving dementia as a separate category. In that year, they received forty-two notifications in this category (1 percent of the total number of notifications in that year).[144] In 2022, the number had gone up to 288 (3.3 percent).[145] Since 2012, the numbers have been increasing in absolute and relative terms. From 2012 to 2022, 1,612 life-termination cases were reported in this category; in 28 of these cases, the procedure was performed on the basis of a written advance directive.

By 2019, the need for clarity was apparent from the relatively large number of judgments (98) in the dementia category published on the website of the review committees and the relatively large number of notified cases (4) that were found to be at odds with the statutory due care criteria.[146] Obviously, the Supreme Court felt that the disparity between the judgments of both disciplinary boards and of the criminal court in the Coffee Euthanasia case did not contribute to the guidance of physicians.

Nevertheless, the Supreme Court's rulings at least brought about some certainty. Physicians considering whether or not to act upon a written euthanasia request will have been somewhat reassured. The Court unequivocally established that it is up to them to interpret the written advance directive, whereby all of the circumstances of the case will have to be considered, and not just the literal wording of the advance directive, to determine the patient's intentions.

Finally, by ruling that the question of whether the physician performing the euthanasia has acted in compliance with the due care criteria should be assessed based on the insights and guidelines of the medical professional, the criminal courts have been made to understand that they should exercise caution. And the Public Prosecutor's Office has also been sent the clear message not to pursue criminal prosecution too lightly.

3.4.2 Interpreting Euthanasia Law

However, some critical comments are warranted. The Coffee Euthanasia case hinges entirely on interpretation, on the interpretation of the advance directive and on the interpretation of the Euthanasia Act's provision on written advance directives. In the first sentence of the latter provision, two capabilities are mentioned: the capability to express one's will and the capability to appraise one's interests reasonably. The absence of the first capability is required when a physician is considering whether or not to comply with the written advance directive. In contrast, the second capability needs to be present when that directive is being drafted. It is up to physicians to reconcile both parts of that sentence in their decision-making. A literal interpretation of the sentence would require a reticent attitude on their part as regards written euthanasia requests by demented patients. After all, only a profoundly comatose patient is entirely unable to express anything. In the Coffee Euthanasia case, the euthanasia review committee, the Public Prosecutor's Office, the Inspectorate, and both disciplinary boards took this position.

On the other hand, the geriatrician's interpretation of that sentence made her feel confident enough to declare that she would have performed euthanasia even if her patient had indicated she did not want her life ended.[147] The criminal court clearly favored this interpretation. The practical implications of the different interpretations are enormous. But which interpretation is the correct one?

As discussed in Section 3.1.3, the Supreme Court based its judgment in the criminal case solely on legislative history. The reference list of its rulings consists of just a few references to parliamentary documents that are more than twenty years old.

Now, the Euthanasia Act is a text first and foremost, and legal texts have in common with many other "public" texts that the original intention of the empirical author is not particularly relevant for a proper understanding. Like literary works, legal texts are produced for a community of readers. The empirical author of a public text knows its readers will not necessarily interpret it in accordance with the author's original intent.[148] A published novel is not a secret diary, with the author and reader being the same person. Nor is it a personal letter, with a recipient who could contact the sender and ask them what they meant. A law is no different, even when the author has left many notes about what was intended in the form of parliamentary documents. Once released to the public, the text of the law is what we must hold on to.[149]

On the other hand, a legal text cannot have every meaning attributed to it by its readers. A text is not a picnic, as Umberto Eco once said, to which the words are taken by its author and its meaning by its readers.[150] A text can have multiple meanings but does not allow for all interpretations. Some are acceptable, and others are not. A text has meaning in itself. An assertion about what Eco calls its *intentio operis* can only be proved by placing it alongside the text as a coherent whole. Any interpretation of one of its parts can be accepted if it is confirmed by other parts of the text, just as any interpretation given thereof must be rejected if it contradicts them. The more that part is confirmed, the more acceptable its interpretation is.[151] The most acceptable interpretation is the one – using Ronald Dworkin's terminology – with the best "fit."[152] Did the Supreme Court provide such an interpretation of the first sentence of the Act's provision on written advance directives? Did it come up with the most acceptable interpretation? Has it succeeded in finding its *intentio operis*?

Suppose that on these pages I suggest to readers an interpretation of an enigmatic passage in *Foucault's Pendulum* by Umberto Eco, a passage to be found in chapter 107 of that book. And suppose I then claim this interpretation to be the correct one. However, if I subsequently add that I have only read that chapter, my claim will hardly be taken seriously by readers who are familiar with this 120-chapter novel. Such an interpretative strategy will startle many. An interpretation of a part of a text would indeed have to be based on an understanding of the entire text as a coherent whole. And what applies to literary criticism also applies to law. The entire text needs to be read and understood as a coherent whole, a text which – unlike Eco's bulky novel – is written by countless authors.

As regards the first analogical application of the regulatory concept, it is essential to realize that the Dutch law on euthanasia is not solely made up of the Euthanasia Act. The Burial and Cremation Act is also relevant, as are provisions of the Criminal Code on termination of life on request and assisted suicide, which are in turn embedded in fundamental rights protected by the Dutch Constitution and numerous European and international human rights treaties to which the Netherlands is a party. Again, no references to fundamental rights are made in either of the Supreme Court's rulings in the Coffee Euthanasia case. It should have spoken out clearly on how the Act's provision concerning written advance directives relates to those points of reference. The Supreme Court should have come up with a coherent understanding of the entirety of Dutch euthanasia law. It should have grasped its underlying principles, produced a sound theory of all applicable rules, and presented an interpretation of the provision that best fits that theory.

The Supreme Court may very well have come up with the most acceptable interpretation, but it has failed to provide proof. It simply did not read the entire book on Dutch euthanasia law. It skipped the chapter on fundamental rights.

3.4.3 No Basis in Statute Law

Unwillingness to "read the entire book" is also apparent in the second analogical application of the regulatory concept. The Order establishing the Review Committee on Late-term Abortions and Termination of Life in Newborns is a ministerial regulation issued jointly by the health and justice ministers. Unlike those of the Euthanasia Act, its rules are not laid down in statute law.[153]

In the Netherlands, fundamental rights are protected in two ways. The Netherlands is a party to numerous international and European human rights treaties. In addition, the Dutch Constitution of the Kingdom of the Netherlands contains a catalog of fundamental rights. Although it does not have provisions on the right to life, the Constitution does safeguard the right to physical integrity. Article 11 reads: "Everyone has the right to the inviolability of their body, subject to limitations to be set by or under the law." However, all liberties protected by the Dutch Constitution are "subject to limitations set by or under the law." For restrictions on exercising the right to physical integrity, statute law or regulation based on statute law is required. Constitutionally, either the legislator issues restrictive rules, or another body granted regulatory power by the legislator does. However, the legislator did not come up with such rules, nor did it grant such a power to another body. The Order establishing the Review Committee on Late-Term Abortions and Termination of Life in Newborns is a set of rules without any basis in statute law. The Dutch legislator has failed to fulfill its constitutional obligations. The Order (including its predecessor) has been evaluated twice. In the latest study report, the legislator was urged to provide statute law.[154]

Policymakers also appear unwilling to bring fundamental rights into the equation. However, they must respect the integrity of the law as well. And since the proposed rules on termination of life in children aged between one and twelve are nothing but an addition to the existing Order, the chapter on fundamental rights will likely be ignored again.

3.4.4 Too Hard to Fit in?

From a fundamental rights point of view, the second and third analogical applications of the regulatory concept, especially, are challenging. Being a party to numerous human rights treaties, the Netherlands is obliged to harmonize its laws and rules with their provisions. As far as the performance of euthanasia on children is concerned, the legal framework provided for by the ECHR is supplemented by provisions to be found in the Convention on the Rights of the Child (CRC). The most relevant are:

- Article 6: States Parties recognize that every child has the inherent right to life. States Parties shall ensure, to the maximum extent possible, the survival and development of the child.
- Article 3: In all actions concerning children ... the best interests of the child shall be a primary consideration.
- Article 4: States Parties shall undertake all appropriate ... measures for the implementation of the rights recognized in the present Convention. Regarding economic, social, and cultural rights, States Parties shall undertake such measures to the maximum extent of their available resources.
- Article 23: States Parties recognize that a mentally or physically disabled child should enjoy a full and decent life .... States Parties acknowledge the right of the disabled child to special care.
- Article 24: States Parties recognize the right of the child to the enjoyment of the highest attainable standard of health and to facilities for the treatment of illness and rehabilitation of health.[155]

As discussed in Section 3.1.4, the right to life is also protected by the ECHR. According to Article 2, everyone's right to life is protected by law. Although the right to life is not absolute, the permissible interferences by the state with exercising that right are extremely limited in number. For this reason, the right to life enjoys a special status among the rights and freedoms protected by the ECHR.

The state party to the ECHR is not merely obliged to abstain from acts violating the right to life. It also has a positive obligation to take measures to protect everyone's right to life. To that end, it must have rules prohibiting deprivation of life backed by effective enforcement. Traditionally, criminal law has been the only appropriate instrument as far as intentional ending of human life is concerned.[156] However, since the ECtHR's ruling in the case of *Pretty* v. *United Kingdom* (2002), intentional ending of life on request by the person concerned is considered to be the exception. Because of that ruling, states that are party to the ECHR are no longer obliged to make such acts punishable by law. As regards the total ban on assisted suicide in the United Kingdom, the European Court stated that "[Mrs. Pretty] is prevented by law from exercising her choice to avoid what she considers will be an undignified and distressing end to her life. The Court is not prepared to exclude that this constitutes an interference with her right to respect for private life."[157]

In *Haas* v. *Switzerland* (2011), the European Court clarified that "an individual's right to decide by what means and at what point his or her life will end, provided he or she is capable of freely reaching a decision on this question and acting in consequence, is one of the aspects of the right to respect for private life within the meaning of Article 8 of the Convention."[158] Consequently, interferences by public authorities with the exercise of that right must meet the requirements of Article 8, paragraph 2. They must be in accordance with the law, meet a pressing social need, and be proportional to one of the legitimate aims mentioned in that paragraph. And protection of the right to life (of those incapable of freely reaching a decision about what means and at what point their lives will end), as enshrined in Article 2, is such a legitimate aim.

However, the Order establishing the Review Committee on Late-Term Abortions and Termination of Life in Newborns is not about intentional termination of life and of weighing the right to privacy against the right to life. The Order and the proposed amendment are about intentional termination of life in incompetent human beings, that is, without request. No leeway is given by the ECtHR regarding the intentional ending of life without request. In its ruling in *Haas* v. *Switzerland*, the Court added,

> Article 2 of the Convention . . . creates for the authorities a duty to protect vulnerable persons, even against actions by which they endanger their own lives . . . . For the Court, this latter Article obliges the national authorities to prevent an individual from taking his or her own life if the decision has not been taken freely and with a full understanding of what is involved.[159]

And, as with all fundamental rights protected by the ECHR, their enjoyment may not be merely "theoretical or illusory."[160]

In March 2007 the predecessor of the current Order took effect. Curiously, this regulation only addressed the establishment of a national review committee. The due care requirements could be found in the explanatory memorandum.[161]

During its evaluation, which took place in 2013, it turned out that the regulation was inadequate. There was almost no reporting because of a lack of clarity regarding the due care requirements, especially concerning the criterion of suffering, and because of a lack of trust among physicians.[162]

As a result, the regulation was replaced by the current one. Four changes were made. First, the requirements of due care were included in the regulation itself. Second, the composition of the committee was changed. From now on, it would consist of six members instead of five (four doctors, an ethicist, and a lawyer), with the chair no longer automatically being the lawyer.[163] Third, the Public Prosecutor's instruction was renewed. The expert committee's judgment would no longer be just advice to the prosecutor; it would be a "weighty" one.[164] In effect, the prosecutor's judgment thus became a settlement judgment. And finally, the concept of suffering was broadened, not in the regulation itself but in the explanatory memorandum:

> Because the doctor must have been convinced that there is unbearable and hopeless suffering, in principle, only the actual suffering of the newborn is the starting point for a decision to terminate life. However, there are situations where the newborn does not suffer unbearably and hopelessly all the time but does so regularly. Even in cases where there is no hopeless and unbearable suffering at the time of the decision to terminate the baby's life, but where this can be expected with a certain degree of certainty, the review committee may consider termination of life prudent. It is conceivable that a decision to terminate a patient's life will be made in such cases, to prevent unbearable and hopeless suffering, even if there is no actual suffering at the time.[165]

This addition was the result of a position paper adopted by the Royal Dutch Medical Association in 2013, which included the following: "The prognosis regarding the current and future state of health is the basis for the decision to discontinue a life-prolonging decision. In doing so, the physician can consider the expectations regarding the degree of suffering, the severity of the treatment program, the life expectancy, the possibilities for self-reliance, and the degree of dependence on the medical care system."[166] The Review Committee accordingly adopted a definition of termination of life in newborns in its annual reports, as discussed in Section 3.2.2.

Increasingly, the pediatric profession has successfully kept criminal law at bay. However, the amended rules for termination of life in newborns have not led to more notifications. There is little reason to suppose the extension to those aged between one and twelve will be successful in this respect. Presumably, neonatologists and pediatricians would like to see a review procedure similar to the one in the Euthanasia Act. However, by effectively reducing the prosecutor's judgment to a settlement judgment, the enjoyment of the right to life for severely suffering children up to twelve years of age is already made "theoretical or illusory." *Force majeure* is a typical criminal law concept. Standardizing *force majeure* in the sense of emergency as a conflict of duties such that people contemplating a criminal offense can know in advance when they can do so with impunity is very peculiar. From a fundamental rights point of view, almost categorical impunity is not problematic as far as the Euthanasia Act itself is concerned, because it involves requests by competent persons. It is a very different situation when it comes to euthanasia being performed on incompetent children. Legally speaking, such arrangements are most likely a bridge too far.

Regarding the CRC, the Netherlands has not signed and ratified the Optional Protocol to the Convention on the Rights of the Child on a Communications Procedure.[167] Therefore, communications by or on behalf of an individual or group of individuals claiming to be victims of a violation by the Netherlands of the rights outlined in the CRC cannot be submitted to the Committee on the Rights of the Child. However, as a party to the CRC, the Netherlands is duty bound to submit to the Committee reports on the measures it has adopted which give effect to the rights recognized in the CRC and on the progress made on the enjoyment of those rights.[168] In its concluding observations on the fourth periodic report, the Committee expressed its remaining concern that euthanasia can be applied to patients under the age of eighteen.[169]

4 Euthanasia by Nonphysicians

From a legal point of view, it is only proper to understand Dutch euthanasia law as a fundamental rights issue. Historically, however, the Euthanasia Act was not the outcome of discussions on euthanasia as an issue of fundamental rights. First and foremost, it was meant to cater to the needs of attending physicians confronted with patients requesting termination of life or assisted suicide. Over the years, the concept of *force majeure* was fleshed out so that euthanasia became an act of privileged compassion. That the Act's rules are nonetheless largely compatible with the right to privacy as protected by the ECHR is due to the margin of appreciation accepted by the ECtHR in later rulings on assisted suicide. The extent to which euthanasia is conceived as privileged compassion became apparent when the Act's regulatory model was subsequently applied to other patient groups. The unwillingness of Dutch policymakers and courts of law to take notice of relevant fundamental rights is striking, as such rights constitute the backbone of the legal system.

The Order establishing the Review Committee on Late-Term Abortions and Termination of Life in Newborns, and the proposed amendment, make it particularly challenging to see Dutch euthanasia law as a coherent whole.

The position of the European Court on withdrawal of treatment is clear, and also where children are concerned, as was demonstrated by its decisions in the cases of Charlie Gard (who was eleven months old at the time of death) in 2017 and Archie Battersbee (aged twelve) in 2022.[170] Withdrawal of treatment, including life-sustaining treatment, is not at odds with the right to life as protected by Article 2 of the ECHR so long as certain conditions are met.[171] However, the Order and the proposed amendment are not about withdrawing treatment. The Court is also not likely to leave a margin of appreciation to national authorities since there is almost a complete consensus among Council of Europe member states regarding rules making intentional termination of life in incompetent children possible. The Netherlands is the only member state having such rules. There is yet another way to illustrate the extent to which euthanasia is a privileged affair in the Netherlands, as we shall see in this section.

4.1 Heringa (2018)

On January 31, 2018, Albert Heringa received a suspended sentence of six months imprisonment by the Dutch Court of Appeal.[172] This ruling brought an end to a story that began in June 2008 with the suicide of his stepmother. After the District Court had found Mr. Heringa guilty of assisting in suicide in 2013, without imposing any penalty or measure,[173] the Court of Appeal subsequently ruled that his actions were not punishable because of *force majeure* in the sense of emergency.[174] In 2017, the Supreme Court reversed this ruling, and the case was referred to another appellate court.[175] During the trial, the focus was on Mr. Heringa's invocation of *force majeure*.

4.1.1 The Facts

Mr. Heringa's ninety-nine-year-old stepmother ("Moek") resided in a nursing home. She was bedridden and suffered from heart failure. In addition, she had severe back pain and could barely see. Repeatedly, Moek had let it be known she was done with living. Because her general practitioner was not yet willing to help her fulfill her wish to die, Mr. Heringa contacted the Dutch Association for a Voluntary End to Life (NVVE) on behalf of his stepmother. One of its consultants visited Mrs. Heringa and suggested her wish could be carried out by voluntarily refusing food and fluids. This was not what Moek wanted, and when Mr. Heringa discovered his stepmother was collecting pills to carry out her wish to die of her own accord, he felt duty bound to find out how he could help her end her life. Thus, Mr. Heringa obtained a booklet from the Foundation for Scientific Research on Suicide with Care (WOZZ), which provided infor-mation on different methods of suicide. In the three weeks preceding her death, he and his stepmother agreed on when the suicide would occur and how it would be realized – by taking medication, including malaria tablets provided by Mr. Heringa and the pills Moek had collected already. At her express request, Mr. Heringa gave his stepmother these drugs in June 2008, which she swallowed in his presence, whereupon she died.

Parts of the procedure were videotaped by Mr. Heringa, including a conversation in which his stepmother said she was done with her life. These recordings were broadcast on national television in February 2008 as part of a documentary entitled *Moek's Last Wishes: A Self-Directed Death*. Mr. Heringa was subsequently charged with assisting in suicide.

4.1.2 The District Court and the Court of Appeal

Mr. Heringa invoked *force majeure* in the sense of emergency. He felt that he was forced to choose from mutually conflicting duties and interests, and in doing so, he let the most serious prevail. The obligation to comply with Article 294, paragraph 2 of the Criminal Code was at odds with the unwritten moral duty to help his ninety-nine-year-old stepmother achieve a painless, peaceful, dignified death. Mr. Heringa believed he had carefully weighed his options and had observed the principles of proportionality and subsidiarity. In his opinion, there were no real alternatives. Mr. Heringa's stepmother could not obtain the required medication herself and expressly did not choose to die by refusing to eat and drink. In his opinion, consulting her own general practitioner once again or a second general practitioner was not an option either, given the circumstances. Moek did not want to consult another doctor. The fact that she lived in a predominantly Orthodox Protestant region would also have made it difficult to find a willing physician. Finally, Mr. Heringa argued that at that time (spring 2008), such requests to doctors were pointless anyway in situations like that of his stepmother.

According to the District Court, it was unlikely that there were no real alternatives available in advance for realizing the self-chosen end of Mr. Heringa's stepmother's life in a dignified manner. In its opinion, he had made insufficient effort to act within the framework of the Euthanasia Act, whereby statutory requirements of due care could be observed. Mr. Heringa was wrong in qualifying his stepmother's general practitioner as being reluctant and in considering seeking another doctor as futile from the outset. No penalty was imposed because the District Court felt it was beyond question that his actions were also inspired by compassion, given the close bond between Moek and her stepson.[176]

The Court of Appeal also recognized that the Euthanasia Act's special ground of impunity in Article 294, paragraph 2, in conjunction with Article 293, paragraph 2 of the Criminal Code, does not exclude a successful appeal by a nonphysician to Article 40 of the Criminal Code, the Code's general provision on *force majeure*. But, unlike the District Court, the appellate court did accept the appeal to *force majeure* in the sense of emergency. It ruled that Mr. Heringa found himself in actual concrete distress because of the conflict of duties he experienced. The judgment is of interest because the appellate court used the Euthanasia Act's due care requirements as a frame of reference and subsequently concluded that the exceptional circumstances required for a successful appeal to *force majeure* did indeed exist.[177]

4.1.3 The Supreme Court

In cassation, the Public Prosecutor first argued that the Court of Appeal had erred concerning the applicable framework of reference. In doing so, it had misinterpreted the law. According to the Public Prosecutor, the appellate court had also failed to substantiate why Mr. Heringa was entitled to a successful appeal to *force majeure* in the sense of emergency.[178] Without much ado, the Supreme Court agreed:

> In its assessment of the defendant's actions, the Court of Appeal essentially did no more than use as a frame of reference the requirements of due care applicable to a physician, although the defendant was not a physician – which is crucial given the current legislation. Given this . . ., it is incomprehensible that the Court of Appeal has found the appeal to force majeure in the present case to be well-founded, which can only be accepted in very exceptional circumstances. This is not because . . . the defendant did not even meet the requirements of the framework used by the Court.[179]

What exactly was meant by the last sentence is not entirely clear. Still, it is a fact that Mr. Heringa had not reported his actions after his stepmother's death, as doctors are required to do.[180] In contrast, the appellate court had previously concluded that he had "done everything possible to record his actions transparently and thus to make his actions fully verifiable, also for the criminal court."[181] Interestingly, the Supreme Court also considered that restraint as regards the acceptance of *force majeure* in the sense of emergency by a nonphysician was appropriate in light of the social and political debate currently taking place on termination of life on request and assistance in suicide.[182]

4.1.4 Another Appellate Court

Once the Supreme Court had clarified how the law was to be interpreted, it referred the case to another appellate court, which dismissed Mr. Heringa's appeal to *force majeure*. In this respect, several findings were considered relevant: (1) In his final decision, Mr. Heringa allowed himself to be solely led by his stepmother's wishes; he had not sufficiently taken into account that his actions constituted a criminal offense; (2) Mr. Heringa had not asked the NVVE counselor whether he knew of another physician who might be willing to cooperate; and (3) Mr. Heringa had left his stepmother alone after he had helped her take the drugs on the evening of her death.

This last circumstance clearly influenced the sentencing. Not only could there have been unexpected complications during his stepmother's process of dying; the Court considered this course of action to also contradict the reasons for his actions Mr. Heringa brought forward afterward – that he wanted to prevent his stepmother from taking her own life without anyone being present and without her being able to say goodbye to her loved ones beforehand. This course of action had previously been considered justifiable by the first appellate court.[183] Mr. Heringa's departure, as well as his failure to report the unnatural death of his stepmother, had met with understanding at that court, given his stepmother's wish to end her life quietly.[184]

In the end, Albert Heringa received a more severe penalty than had been asked for by the prosecution: a suspended prison sentence of six months with a two-year probation period. Mr. Heringa also brought up another ground for dismissal by arguing that Article 294, paragraph 2 of the Criminal Code should be declared inapplicable due to conflict with Article 8, paragraph 1 of the ECHR. In response, the second appellate court pointed out that according to European case law, the right to privacy does not imply a state obligation to facilitate euthanasia. Within the margin of appreciation, states are free to provide further rules on making euthanasia possible, as long as the requirements set out in Article 8, paragraph 2 of the ECHR are met. Therefore, the appellate court continued, "It falls within the margin of appreciation of a state to determine in which cases it is justified to make an exception to a prohibition on assistance in suicide."[185] And this, it concluded, "implies that it is not in violation of Article 8 ECHR to permit assisted suicide only under the conditions set out in Article 293, paragraph 2 of the Criminal Code, to which the second sentence of Article 294, paragraph 2 of the Criminal Code refers."[186]

4.2 Done with Living

The Supreme Court was clearly unwilling to award the appeal to *force majeure* that doctors can make to a nonphysician. Only in very exceptional circumstances could nonphysicians, in its opinion, appeal to *force majeure* in the sense of emergency as a conflict of duties. But, of course, this is inherent to *force majeure* in this sense; it can only be successfully invoked in very exceptional circumstances. Doctors, however, do not have to make do with the conventional concept of *force majeure* as emergency. In its judgment in the Heringa case, the Supreme Court made it blatantly clear that euthanasia is reserved for doctors only. Notably, a Dutch court of law did include European human rights law in its considerations on this occasion, but only – it seemed – to emphasize the exclusive competence of doctors in this respect. In the Netherlands, euthanasia is indeed an act of privileged compassion.

In its ruling, the Supreme Court also expressed its wish to exercise restraint in view of an ongoing social and political debate. The debate it referred to is the so-called completed-life debate.[187]

4.2.1 Drion's Pill (1991)

The personal choice of elderly people as regards the end of their lives has been the subject of public debate in the Netherlands for quite some time. The discussion was triggered in 1991 by former Supreme Court Justice Huib Drion, who published a controversial essay entitled "The Self-Chosen Death of Elderly People" in which he expressed his conviction that "many elderly would find immense peace of mind if they were to have at their disposal the means of ending their lives in an acceptable manner at the moment this – in view of what life might have in store for them – seems appropriate to them."[188] In his essay, the author advocated what would later become known as Drion's Pill: a substance enabling elderly people to end their lives when they want to, in a manner acceptable to them and the people around them, and obtainable from their general practitioner or from another physician appointed for this purpose.[189]

4.2.2 A Citizens' Initiative (2010)

The debate intensified at the time of the Brongersma case in 2002. Since the Supreme Court's ruling seemed to limit the scope of the Euthanasia Act, advocates of Drion's Pill started exploring other avenues. In 2010, a group called Free Will (*Uit Vrije Wil*) launched a so-called citizens' initiative.

In the Netherlands, individual citizens can put items on the parliamentary agenda by requesting that parliament discusses a detailed proposal in any policy area and takes a stand. Anyone who is of Dutch nationality and is aged eighteen or over can submit a citizens' initiative. At least 40,000 declarations of support are needed for such an initiative to be debated in parliament.[190] The objective of the Free Will citizens' initiative was to legalize the provision of suicide assistance to elderly people who consider their lives to be completed, at their express request and subject to requirements of due care and verifiability.[191]

According to the Free Will group, the Dutch Constitution guarantees all citizens the right to live according to their own views and preferences and to make decisions accordingly. This freedom extends to life's final stage and life-and-death decisions. The group therefore considers self-determination to be the basis of the initiative: A free person who believes their life to be completed should have the right to choose the time and manner of their own death.[192]

The group argued that we are living longer today, usually to our satisfaction. For various reasons, however, we may, at some point, conclude that the value of our life, and its meaning, have diminished to such an extent that we may prefer death to life. When it becomes clear to us that we cannot change our circumstances in any way, we may conclude that our life is completed: We then want to die in peace and with dignity, preferably in the presence of loved ones. This often requires assistance to prevent the suicide attempt from failing and having horrible consequences for the person concerned, or for others.[193]

It was claimed that the personal freedom to decide on one's death is hardly controversial from a moral point of view, and the Free Will group called attention to the fact that suicide is not prohibited by law in the Netherlands. Assisting in suicide, however, is prohibited. Free Will therefore believed that it should no longer be punishable to assist in suicide: Elderly Dutch people who wish to die with dignity should be given this opportunity by amending the law. The group believes this implies professional, responsible, and verifiable assistance in suicide.[194]

Free Will proposed a law for assistance in suicide, to be provided by a suicide assistant: a registered care provider with a certificate showing they have satisfied specific training requirements. The suicide assistant should be associated with a Foundation for Suicide Assistance to Elderly People, which (1) selects, trains, and certifies suicide assistants, (2) supports them, (3) develops professional standards for suicide assistance, (4) supervises the prescription of lethal drugs, and (5) periodically assesses the practice of assisted suicide and reports on this to the government.[195]

According to the proposal, elderly people, that is, people aged seventy and over, should direct their requests to suicide assistants, who will not be prosecuted if they comply with the due care requirements and properly report cases where they have provided suicide assistance.[196] When considering a request, suicide assistants must satisfy the following criteria. They must:

    a. be convinced that the request for assistance in suicide is voluntary, well-considered, and persistent;

    b. have established that the request was made by a Dutch citizen or by a citizen of a member state of the European Union who has been a resident for at least two years and that the person who made the request has reached the age of 70;

c. have informed the person who made the request about the substantive and procedural aspects of the requested assistance in suicide;

d. have received a written statement from the person who made the request containing a request for assistance in suicide;

e. have consulted at least one other independent suicide assistant who has spoken to the person making the request and given a written opinion on the due care requirements, as referred to under (a) to (d);

f. ensure that the assistance in suicide is provided in a professional manner.[197]

Under the proposed law, a suicide assistant must notify the municipal coroner and explain how the due care requirements were satisfied. The coroner would then establish how and by what means the patient ended their life and also check whether the report of the suicide assistant was drafted correctly. In turn, the coroner would issue a report on the assisted suicide to one of the five regional euthanasia review committees (set up under the Euthanasia Act), enclosing the relevant documents (the reasoned report of the suicide assistant, and the written opinion of the consulted independent suicide assistant) with their own account.[198]

The regional euthanasia review committees, composed of a suicide assistant, an ethicist, and a lawyer–chairperson, would provide written opinions on the reports they receive. A committee would assess whether the suicide assistant acted in accordance with the due care requirements. If it concluded that the assistant had satisfied all the requirements, this conclusion would be shared with them, and the case would be closed. If it drew another conclusion, the findings would also be shared with the Public Prosecutor's Office and the Healthcare Inspectorate. The Public Prosecutor's Office would subsequently decide whether to initiate criminal proceedings; the Healthcare Inspectorate would see whether other measures should be taken.[199]

The citizens' initiative proposal is clearly modeled after the Euthanasia Act. What distinguishes the proposal from the Act is that a request can only be submitted by someone aged seventy or over. Unlike the Euthanasia Act, the proposal requires that the request is persistent and submitted in writing. Moreover, the suicide assistant does not necessarily need to be a physician. When a case of assisted suicide is reported, another certified suicide assistant will take a seat on the regional euthanasia review committee. Finally, the due care requirements are slightly different. Hopeless and unbearable suffering from a medically classifiable disorder is not required. The suicide assistant also does not have to inform the elderly person about their situation or prospects and reach a conclusion (together with the person concerned) that there was no other reasonable solution to their situation.[200]

4.2.3 The Schnabel Committee (2016)

When the citizens' initiative was submitted to parliament in May 2010, the number of declarations of support had reached 116,871. The parliamentary committees on security and justice and on health, welfare, and sports held a public consultation with the initiators in February 2011. Later that year, parliament also conducted hearings with academics, publicists, lay experts, and relevant civil society organizations. The citizens' initiative was debated in plenary in March 2012.[201]

Parliament ultimately decided against any further discussions on the matter. Nevertheless, it did request the government to have further studies conducted. In July 2014, the health and justice ministers set up a committee to advise them on the social issues and legal options regarding the provision of suicide assistance to people who consider their lives to be completed.[202] The committee – named after its chair Mr. Paul Schnabel – made its recommendations known in February 2016.[203]

The committee was not asked to specifically consider the initiative's proposal. It was to focus on examining "how the wish can be fulfilled of an increasing number of Dutch citizens to be invested with a greater right of self-determination in the form of assistance when they consider their lives to be completed."[204] It was considered to be "of essential importance that misuse be prevented and people feel secure."[205]

Because various terms are used in public and political debates on the issue, such as "completed life," "done with living," "suffering from life," "tired of life," "voluntary euthanasia," and "self-chosen death," the committee first identified a number of characteristic aspects of a "completed life." It then determined that the issue concerned people "who are generally elderly who, in their opinion, no longer have anything to look forward to in their lives, and who have developed an active and persistent wish to die as a result."[206]

The Schnabel committee assigned various subquestions to independent academics. Based on their findings, it distinguished four different "completed life" situations: (1) situations within the scope of the Euthanasia Act, that is, situations characterized by suffering predominantly caused by a medical condition; (2) situations regarded as "borderline cases" because it is less clear whether the suffering is predominantly caused by a medical condition; (3) situations in which there is no suffering due to a medical condition; and (4) situations in which there is no suffering at all.[207]

Because it had not commissioned empirical research, the Schnabel committee assumed that the number of persons considering their lives to be "completed" and who consequently have an active wish to die is probably tiny, especially when the wish to terminate their lives is unrelated to medical problems. It estimated that, in many cases, this wish is based on a medical condition in which a combination of medical and nonmedical issues has resulted in unbearable and hopeless suffering within the meaning of the Euthanasia Act. In other words, most people who are suffering and feel their lives are "completed" can be classified under the first category: They can invoke the Euthanasia Act (without having a claim right, of course). Insofar as people who are suffering and feel that their lives are "completed" fall into the second category, the committee considered that it is up to the regional euthanasia review committees to discover whether the Euthanasia Act is applicable and, if so, to what extent. According to the Schnabel committee, the number of persons who may be classified under the third or fourth categories is very likely too small to justify expanding the legal possibilities regarding assistance in suicide.[208]

The Schnabel committee believed that the Euthanasia Act provides sufficient scope for obviating most problems relating to "completed life." It felt that the Act functions properly and that it fulfills its objectives. It is practiced with due care and enjoys broad support among physicians. Most physicians report euthanasia and assisted suicide cases, ensuring the practice remains transparent and assessable. Furthermore, since the issue relates to life and death, the committee considered physicians' involvement essential. For reasons of due care and safety, a physician simply has to be involved because of their medical expertise in assessing the voluntary and well-considered nature of the patient's request, the availability of alternatives, and the safe and careful performance of euthanasia or the provision of suicide assistance.[209]

Ultimately, further expansion of the legal possibilities for assisted suicide was considered undesirable. Besides being unnecessary, new legislation would probably also adversely affect a practice deemed transparent and carefully conducted.[210]

4.2.4 Mrs. Dijkstra's Bill (2020)

The Schnabel committee did not conduct empirical studies to substantiate its claims. However, another committee commissioned by the health minister did. That committee, the Van Wijngaarden committee (also named after its chair), found the numbers to be very small. Based on a survey held in 2019 (with a sample of 32,477 people aged fifty-five and over; the total population in that age category in the Netherlands at the time was 5.6 million and the number of respondents who returned the questionnaire was 21,294), it estimated that only approximately 1,700 people aged seventy-five and over had a persistent and active desire to end their lives.[211] This small number did not prevent social liberal MP Mrs. Pia Dijkstra from introducing a bill.

In the Netherlands, it is usually the government that proposes new legislation. However, any member of parliament can do so as well. As the citizens'
initiative did not have the desired outcome (a government proposal),
Mrs. Dijkstra started preparing a bill, which she introduced in parliament in
July 2020.[212] Not surprisingly, the Euthanasia Act served as a model once
again. The bill proposes to add a third paragraph to the Criminal Code's ban on
assisting in suicide.[213] Once the proposed End-of-Life Counseling of the
Elderly Act has become law, Article 294 of the Criminal Code will read as
follows:

1. He who intentionally incites another to commit suicide shall, if the
    suicide follows, be punished by imprisonment for a term not exceeding
    three years or a fourth category fine.
2. He who intentionally assists another in suicide or provides them with the
    means to do so shall, if the suicide follows, be punished with imprison-
    ment for a term not exceeding three years or a fine of the fourth category.
    Article 293, paragraph 2, applies mutatis mutandis.
3. *The offense referred to in the second paragraph is not punishable
    if it consists of providing means for suicide and is committed by an
    end-of-life counselor as referred to in the End-of-Life Counseling of
    the Elderly Act who thereby complies with the requirements of care as
    referred to in Article 2 of that Act and notifies the municipal coroner of
    this in accordance with Article 7a, part b, of the Burial and Cremation
    Act* (emphasis added).

The bill is meant to cater to the needs of the elderly. According to the proposal,
an elder is a person aged seventy-five or over.[214] The end-of-life counselor
referred to will be a registered practitioner of a newly created profession.
These practitioners will be qualified experts in end-of-life counseling as
referred to in the proposed act. They might be physicians, nurses, psychother-
apists, or clinical psychologists, but they will have to meet additional training
requirements yet to be specified by the health minister. Once qualified, they
must have enrolled in the registry kept by the health ministry for healthcare
professionals.[215]

The extent to which the bill mimics the Euthanasia Act is quite astounding.
End-of-life counselors considering assisting in suicide must also meet due care
requirements. These can be found in Article 2 of the proposed act:

According to the requirements of care referred to in Article 294, paragraph 3,
of the Dutch Criminal Code, the end-of-life counselor:

a. has established that at the time of receipt of the statement referred to in
    section h, the elder is a Dutch citizen or has been a resident of the Netherlands
    for at least two years;

b. has asked the elder whether they involved their next of kin in their request for assisted suicide and, if they have not yet done so but it is still possible to do so, has suggested that they do so;

c. if possible and in so far as the elder has consented, has consulted the elder's general practitioner;

d. has come to the conviction that it is a voluntary, well-considered, and permanent request, whereby at least two months have elapsed between successive talks with the elder;

e. has come to the conviction with the elder that other help, given the background of the request, is not desirable;

f. has determined that the individual is an elder who is capable of a reasonable evaluation of their interests in the matter and has received from them a demonstrably current statement, recorded in writing or by audiovisual means, including a request to provide them with the means for their intended suicide;

g. has informed the elder of the substantive and procedural aspects of assisted suicide;

h. has consulted at least one other independent end-of-life counselor who has seen the elder and has given their opinion in writing regarding compliance with the requirements for care referred to in parts a through g;

i. ensures that the assisted suicide is carried out in a professional manner, which in any case includes compliance with the provisions of Chapter 3, except for Article 4, paragraph 2.[216]

Once these requirements have been met, the counselor and the elder concerned agree on the time of the intended suicide.[217] At that time, the counselor will provide the latter with the necessary drugs.[218] The proposed Act also requires the counselor to attend the elder's suicide.[219]

The Burial and Cremation Act is amended to accommodate a notification procedure identical to the one to be followed by physicians performing termination of life on request or assisting in suicide in accordance with the Euthanasia Act.[220] The municipal coroner subsequently informs the competent regional euthanasia review committee,[221] which will review in the way prescribed by the Euthanasia Act.[222] However, its composition is slightly different; a registered end-of-life counselor replaces the physician.[223] Finally, the Public Prosecutor's Office and the Healthcare Inspectorate are only informed if the committee finds that the counselor has not acted in accordance with the proposed act's due care requirements.[224]

Mrs. Dijkstra's bill is a well-thought-out successor to the citizens' initiative. Numerous references to the initiative are made in the accompanying explanatory memorandum. The proposed law is meant to broaden the legal possibilities for assisted suicide for the elderly who consider their lives to be completed.[225]

Although the proposal is said to be based on several principles (respect for human life, quality of life, dying with dignity, solidarity, compassion, and tolerance), one in particular stands out:

> The basic premise of this bill is that, in principle, everyone should have the freedom to organize their own lives as they see fit. This does not only mean shaping one's own life, but also, for example, being able and being allowed to decide about one's own body and, by extension, about one's own life, which is, after all, inextricably linked to the body. This right also includes being able to make decisions about the last phase of life and thus about one's own end of life. Everyone has the right to stop living; conversely, no one has a duty to live or continue. Older people themselves also associate this self-determination ... with the self-chosen end of life.[226]

This basic premise is not shared with the Euthanasia Act. However, since dying with dignity cannot do without the involvement of others, nor that of society as a whole, self-determination or autonomy is not presented by Mrs. Dijkstra as an absolute principle concerning only the individual interests of the elderly. In the accompanying explanatory memorandum, autonomy is not presented as a claimable right others must meet. Therefore, as a right, self-determination does not correspond with a duty on the part of others or the government to assist in suicide.[227] The End-of-Life Counseling of the Elderly Act will not create a right to assistance in suicide, should the bill ever pass – a feature it shares with the Euthanasia Act.

4.3 The Autonomous Route

In Dutch debates on euthanasia, the regulatory model provided by the Euthanasia Act appears almost unavoidable. It seems impossible to conceive of other means of regulation – the model is always followed in one way or another. Nevertheless, referring to it does not come naturally to everyone, especially not to those who unreservedly put autonomy forward as the only relevant principle.

The Last Will Cooperative (*Coöperatie Laatste Wil*, with approximately 22,000 members) is a Dutch advocacy organization. According to its charter, the Cooperative primarily devotes itself to "furnishing last-will substances to members of the cooperative to enable them to accomplish termination of their own lives, by their own choice and by taking matters into their own hands, at a time to be selected by themselves, without any third-party verification, and in accordance with the law."[228] It purports to be concerned "with the availability of safe, humane and legal means and an atmosphere of openness and transparency in which the autonomous route can be taken."[229]

Since its foundation in 2013, the Cooperative has primarily advocated the abolition of Article 294, paragraph 2 of the Criminal Code, which prohibits assisting suicide. In September 2017, however, the Cooperative announced that it knew of a certain powder that it claimed was highly suitable for suicide, a freely obtainable substance, although it was intended for an entirely different purpose. The organization did not disclose the name of this substance, although it stated that only two grams of the powder would suffice.[230] Within only a short period of time, tens of thousands of people contacted the organization. The first 1,000 were meant to have the lethal powder (known as Drug X, presumably sodium azide) sent to them in April 2018.

The announcement provoked much criticism, particularly after a nineteen-year-old woman had taken her own life using a powder she had purchased online, which she had probably identified on the basis of information provided by the Cooperative.[231] In March 2018, the Cooperative reported that a number of its members actually intended to purchase the powder to distribute it among other members. Those who ordered individual portions of this product could keep it in their homes in a special safe, which they could also purchase.[232] After it became clear this meant that an anticipated 1,000 persons would have this substance in their possession in the very near future, the Public Prosecutor's Office instituted criminal investigations into the Cooperative's actions. It also strongly urged the organization to cease its operations immediately.[233] In March 2018, the Cooperative announced its intention to suspend purchasing the substance. Because it was unwilling to risk criminal prosecution, it ceased providing information on the lethal powder.[234]

Although the organization had reduced its activities to sharing information among its members about euthanasia products and ways to obtain them, three of its members were arrested in 2021 on suspicion of having provided lethal drugs to assist with suicide.[235] On July 18, 2023, one individual, known as Alex S., was sentenced to three-and-a-half years in prison, eighteen months of which was suspended with a two-year probation period.[236] According to the District Court, Alex S. distributed Drug X "in a businesslike manner."[237] Between 2018 and 2021, he sold it to about 1,600 people. At least ten of them actually used the drug to end their lives. The Court noted that Alex S. had "little regard for the lives of others and caused damage to the value of human life in general." Because of his surreptitious dealing, the judges added, "a large amount of a lethal drug is present in society," and "no supervision or control of its use is possible."[238]

In 2022, the Last Will Cooperative also filed a civil lawsuit against the state. Referring to Article 8 of the ECHR, its lawyers argued that the Netherlands acted unlawfully by fully enforcing the prohibition on assisted suicide. However, on December 14, 2022, the District Court found that with article 294, paragraph 2 of the Criminal Code and the associated procedure of the Euthanasia Act, the State has struck a careful balance ("fair balance") between, on the one hand, the social interests served by the criminal law prohibition on assisted suicide (protection of life, prevention of abuse and protection of vulnerable persons) and, on the other hand, the interest of the individual to receive assistance in suicide by a doctor in cases of unbearable and hopeless suffering.[239]

Therefore, combined with the Euthanasia Act, the ban on assisted suicide in Article 294, paragraph 2 of the Criminal Code was not considered disproportionate. The Court subsequently concluded that the state did not act unlawfully toward the Cooperative and its supporters by fully enforcing the prohibition. To the extent that it constitutes an interference with the right to respect for private life, as protected by Article 8 of the ECHR, of those to whom the Euthanasia Act does not apply, the Court considered this interference justified on the basis of Article 8, paragraph 2 of the ECHR.[240]

4.4 More Preliminary Observations

Judging by the number of declarations of support the Free Will group managed to collect and also by the membership numbers of organizations such as the Dutch Voluntary Euthanasia Association and the Last Will Cooperative, the options offered by the Euthanasia Act are not considered sufficient by many. The principles of euthanasia legislation have been debated in the Netherlands since the early 1990s. There are those who argue that personal autonomy rather than privileged compassion should be the guiding principle. Thus far, there has been little reception to this idea by courts of law and policymakers. Albert Heringa was convicted of assisting in suicide, the citizens' initiative led to nothing, the Public Prosecutor's Office closely monitors the activities of the Last Will Cooperative, and it remains to be seen whether anything will ever come of Mrs. Dijkstra's bill. On the other hand, the notion of euthanasia as an act of privileged compassion has received approval, even to the extent that the Euthanasia Act's model is (about to be) applied in ways that are extremely difficult to reconcile with fundamental rights.

Except for those advocating the autonomous route, proponents of further decriminalization of assistance in suicide have argued their case by suggesting further analogical applications of the regulatory concept. The rules are embedded in criminal law, due care requirements need to be met, and procedures of notification and review by an expert committee are provided. Perhaps Mrs. Dijkstra's proposed law is not very imaginative, but the success of the example provided by the Euthanasia Act happens to be unparalleled. As far as fundamental rights protection is concerned, it is undoubtedly a match for the latter. Constitutionally, the state is not duty bound to facilitate assisting in suicide. Physical integrity and respect for privacy are fundamental rights guaranteed by the Dutch Constitution. Still, the relevant constitutional provisions do not indicate how assisting suicide should be regulated if the choice was made to facilitate it. They simply state that limitations must be set by or under the law. Once passed, Mrs. Dijkstra's rules will meet this requirement.

The ECHR poses even less of an obstacle. In *Haas* v. *Switzerland*, the European Court acknowledged that the right to respect for private life encompasses deciding when and how to die. Restrictions on this right are allowed too, but they must be provided for by law (which means that the restriction must be sufficiently recognizable and foreseeable). They must be necessary in a democratic society (meet a pressing social need, be proportionate, and appropriate) in the light of the legitimate aims mentioned in Article 8, paragraph 2 of the ECHR, which include the protection of the rights and freedoms of others. In determining what is necessary for a democratic society to serve these aims, the ECHR leaves a "margin of appreciation" to member states, which tends to be broad if the ECtHR cannot establish consensus among those states as regards the scope of the fundamental right concerned or its restrictions. Since the margin is likely to be broad, given its rulings on assisted suicide, it is safe to say that the proposed End-of-Life Counseling of the Elderly Act will not be at odds with ECHR provisions. Provided that the state fulfills its obligation to protect the lives of those who are not competent to decide when and how to die, that condition also applies to the Euthanasia Act.

The KNMG did not welcome the citizens' initiative and Mrs. Dijkstra's bill. As regards the proposed End-of-Life Counseling of the Elderly Act, it expressed its concern about the relationship with the Euthanasia Act.[241] The Association feared the new law would subvert existing euthanasia practice. Why would people aged seventy-five and over still take advantage of the opportunities offered by the Euthanasia Act? Why would elderly people suffering hopelessly and unbearably, predominantly because of a medical condition, not opt for the opportunities the proposed law provides?

5 Age-Related Conditions

In 2016, the Schnabel committee advised against introducing a law allowing people who consider their lives completed to be assisted in suicide. It assumed that most people who are suffering and consider their lives completed could already invoke the Euthanasia Act. It estimated that their wish to die, in many cases, stemmed from a combination of medical and nonmedical problems resulting in hopeless and unbearable suffering within the meaning of the

Euthanasia Act. And, insofar as there is doubt about whether suffering is indeed "predominantly" caused by a medically classifiable illness or disorder, the committee stated that it is up to the euthanasia review committees to determine the scope of the Euthanasia Act (Paragraph 4.2.3).

Was the Schnabel committee correct in its assumptions? And what is meant by "suffering predominantly caused by a medically classifiable illness or disorder"? Let us consider the review committees' policy and practice on notifications of euthanasia with regard to patients suffering from multiple geriatric syndromes.

5.1 An Avid Reader

In 2010, when the citizens' initiative brought about intense public debate on the completed life issue, the regional euthanasia review committees came up with several very interesting judgments.[242] One of the reviewed notifications concerned a woman aged eighty-six.[243] She lived independently in her own home, used the internet and email, and thoroughly enjoyed reading on the subjects of philosophy, politics, and art. However, her physical condition was deteriorating, which meant she was increasingly unable to do everything that made her life worth living. For the last few years, her vision had deteriorated, she had become hard of hearing, she suffered from dizziness, and she was incontinent. The woman felt imprisoned by her own body and regarded the termination of her life as a deliverance. She said her life was completed. According to the report, she wanted to end her own life, or have it terminated for her, because she was "suffering from life."[244]

The regional euthanasia review committee resolved to summon the notifying physician to give a verbal explanation. On that occasion, the physician stated that, in retrospect, it was "rather unwise" of her to refer so explicitly to "suffering from life" in the report. The physician explained what she meant: her patient's suffering was caused by her own physical deterioration, and she became increasingly dependent on others as a consequence. The patient's poor vision was due to macular degeneration. The condition of her eyes was unstable, and her eyesight had considerably deteriorated in a very short time. As far as the physician was concerned, the macular degeneration was the reason why she wanted to comply with her patient's request.[245]

When reviewing the notification, the committee extensively discussed whether the patient's situation could be classified as "completed life." The committee considered whether a medical disorder caused the patient's suffering in the present case: "The patient's situation must be characterized as suffering according to medical and ethical standards. Therefore, the suffering must have a medical dimension . . . . A physician cannot form an opinion on suffering resulting from any context other than a medical one; such suffering is outside the physician's field of expertise."[246]

For this reason, the committee referred to the Supreme Court's classification criterion. According to the patient, her suffering was caused to a significant extent by her eyesight becoming poorer. As far as she was concerned, the worst part of it was her gradual loss of autonomy; she became increasingly dependent on others due to her failing eyesight. The committee identified macular degeneration as a medically classifiable disorder for which no effective treatment is available. Therefore, the woman was suffering hopelessly. For this reason, the committee concluded there was no "completed life" situation: The physician's actions were within the medical domain. Given her advanced age, background, and personality, the disorder resulted in unbearable suffering for this patient. In its conclusion, the committee emphasized that the unbearableness of suffering is always a matter of personal experience and that it could only be assessed with restraint. In this particular case, the physician could indeed have concluded that the patient's suffering was unbearable and hopeless.[247]

The facts of the case strongly resemble that of Mr. Brongersma (Section 1.2.7), the difference being that, according to the review committee, the physician had indeed fulfilled all the statutory requirements of due care. The former senator also suffered from various age-related conditions. Although osteoporosis, dizziness, and incontinence are not life-threatening conditions, they could be construed as providing a medical basis for his suffering. But his suffering did not meet the second requirement because it was not "predominantly caused by a medically classifiable illness or disorder," whereas the suffering of the eighty-six-year-old woman did. There is little doubt that if a review committee were to assess Mr. Brongersma's case today, his suffering would qualify as being "predominantly caused by a medically classifiable illness or disorder." The same would probably be true of Mr. Heringa's 99-year-old stepmother's suffering. So, what has happened since the Supreme Court's ruling in the Brongersma case?

5.2 Accumulating Age-Related Conditions and Dimensions of Suffering

It is not uncommon for the elderly to receive medical treatment for dizziness, osteoporosis, incontinence, and so on without any other cause for these disorders other than advanced age. Suffering from an age-related condition is almost by definition hopeless suffering. But what does it take to qualify such suffering as unbearable?

Partly in response to the citizens' initiative, the KNMG published a position paper on the physician's role in self-chosen termination of life in 2011.[248] This paper is relevant for two reasons. First, a reference to "accumulation of age-related conditions" was made in connection with the scope of the Euthanasia Act. The KNMG argued that unbearable and hopeless suffering within the meaning of the Euthanasia Act may be said to exist as a consequence of accumulated age-related conditions, including loss of function, which cause increasing deterioration. However, according to the physicians' association, a medical basis must always exist: a condition that can be identified as an illness, a disorder, or a combination of illnesses or disorders, since this is within the physician's field of expertise.[249]

Second, the KNMG distinguished various "dimensions" of suffering. Research and reporting practice have demonstrated euthanasia to occur most frequently in cases of unbearable suffering caused by somatic problems and complaints. According to the doctors' association, this means that in practice somatic suffering carries the most weight when assessing whether the suffering is actually unbearable. However, it also held that complaints of a psychological, psychosocial, and spiritual nature constitute dimensions of suffering that must be prevented or alleviated using palliative care. Therefore, psychosocial and existential suffering may also be included in the medical domain.[250]

In its paper, the association expected physicians to be confronted far more frequently with vulnerable and increasingly longer-living elderly people who wish to continue living at home for as long as possible. According to the KNMG, one million elderly people in the Netherlands were suffering from multimorbidity in 2011. This number was expected to increase to one-and-a-half million – or almost 10 percent of the Dutch population – within ten years.[251]

Furthermore, it observed that many elderly people suffer from various disorders rendering them vulnerable, although they are not life-threatening. According to the KNMG, "vulnerability" (or "frailty") is synonymous with a simultaneous deterioration – in several areas – of the ability to establish a defense against physical stress and hazards caused by external factors. "Vulnerability" refers to declining physical and mental vitality. Moreover, if an older person is suffering from multimorbidity, this considerably increases the chances of depression, thus increasing their vulnerability. Vulnerability is not only caused by health problems and attendant limitations; it is also related to the extent to which elderly persons possess social skills, financial resources, and social networks. Vulnerability impacts quality of life and the possibility of recovery and may result in unbearable and hopeless suffering. In view of this, it is entirely justifiable – according to the KNMG – for physicians to consider vulnerability (including its various dimensions, such as loneliness, loss of function, and loss of autonomy) when assessing requests for euthanasia.[252]

The KNMG additionally referred to "the non-linear sum and complexity of complaints which are frequently not fatal, and which result in increasing deterioration, which in turn results in an unacceptable existence and thereby in unbearable suffering for the patient."[253] According to the association, this applies to patients who have already frequently undergone substantial physical deterioration over time, exceeding these patients' ability to cope. If, in addition, patients are suffering from visual problems, hearing problems, locomotion problems, being bedridden, exhaustion, and various other complaints and complications, this increases their dependence on others. Consequently, patients will perceive their suffering as unbearable and their existence as pointless. They do not wish to be in a situation where they can no longer give any meaning to their lives in view of their life history and values. In its position paper, the association expressed its firm belief that such cases are linked to the medical domain to such an extent that the actions of a physician performing euthanasia would meet the Euthanasia Act's requirement of suffering.[254]

5.3 The Nature of Suffering

The Dutch government is legally obliged to evaluate the Euthanasia Act every five years. In the second evaluation study, carried out in 2012, it was recommended, inter alia, that the information provided by the committees in their annual reports and anonymized rulings, especially that relating to how they interpret and apply the requirements of due care, should be made more accessible by means of a code of practice. This code materialized in 2015 and provided an overview of the factors the committees consider relevant when reviewing notifications of euthanasia.[255]

The *Code of Practice*, the predecessor of the *Euthanasia Code 2018*, did not devote much attention to the problems relating to "completed life." Its authors merely observed that case law and the legislative process of the Euthanasia Act demonstrated that it is essential for the patient's unbearable suffering to be based on a medical condition.[256] They subsequently stated that there need be no question of any serious or life-threatening disorder, and concluded – thereby referring extensively to the KNMG's position paper – that an accumulation of age-related complaints may also result in unbearable and hopeless suffering.[257]

This point of view was reiterated in the *Euthanasia Code 2018*.[258] The Code also indicated the age-related degenerative conditions that might be relevant in this respect: vision impairment, hearing disorders, osteoporosis, rheumatoid arthritis, balance disorder, and cognitive deterioration. According to the authors, the sum of one or more of these disorders and the relevant ensuing complaints must "give rise to suffering which, in conjunction with the patient's anamnesis, background, personality, values and ability to cope, may be perceived by this particular patient as unbearable and hopeless."[259] How does that pan out?

According to the *Euthanasia Code*, the review committees' own guidelines, the statutory requirement of suffering has two aspects. The patient's suffering is considered to be without any prospect of improvement (or hopeless) if the illness or disorder causing the suffering is incurable and it is impossible to alleviate the symptoms so that the unbearableness disappears. For determining hopelessness, medical opinion is decisive.[260] For this reason, this aspect is seen as objective. The unbearableness of the suffering is considered subjective in that the patient's perceptions predominantly define it.[261] Because unbearableness is difficult to objectify, the review committees assess whether or not this aspect was "understandable" for the physician.[262]

In its Brongersma ruling, the Supreme Court stated that the suffering must be "caused to a significant extent by a medically classifiable (somatic or psychiatric) illness or disorder."[263] It therefore implied that the suffering could also have nonmedical causes. Furthermore, according to the review committees' guidelines, the suffering does not have to be caused by just one illness or disorder. A combination of disorders or illnesses can also cause suffering within the meaning of the Euthanasia Act.[264] And a combination of illnesses or disorders that are not actually life-threatening in and of themselves can also be the cause of the suffering,[265] especially, it would seem, in the case of elderly people. To understand what is meant by suffering being "caused to a significant extent by a medically classifiable illness or disorder," one should analyze those rulings on notifications concerning elderly patients in which nonmedical causes were also identified.[266]

5.3.1 Multiple Geriatric Syndromes

Since 2013, "multiple geriatric syndromes" have been included as a category in the joint annual reports of the Regional Euthanasia Review Committees (see Section 2.1).[267] These judgments relate precisely to cases where the suffering also had nonmedical causes. Up to August 10, 2019, forty-nine such judgments had been published on the joint review committees' website, of which only one led to the conclusion "due care criteria not complied with."[268] The other forty-eight judgments were studied to see what information was given about the nature of the suffering.[269]

According to the annual reports, 1,433 notifications of euthanasia in connection with multiple geriatric syndromes were made from January 1, 2013 to

January 1, 2019. The published judgments are a tiny percentage of the total number of registered notifications in this category up to August 10, 2019.

What the published anonymized judgments say about the review practice of these notifications is unclear. Forty-nine judgments is a tiny number compared to the total number, but they were apparently worthy of attention since the committees decided to publish them. However, the exact reason for their publication is often not revealed.[270] Although it is difficult to determine precisely what is being revealed by publishing these judgments, they are all a researcher has to go on. The vast majority of judgments in this category apparently did not deserve public attention.

The figures in Table 1 do not reveal a discernible trend in the annual number of notifications in the "multiple geriatric syndromes" category, nor do they suggest a growing number of notifications of euthanasia involving elderly people on the basis of nonmedical causes or "completed life" or "completed life"-type arguments since 2013. However, it should be noted that the numbers in the "multiple geriatric syndromes" category have been increasing since 2019, with 217 notifications in 2019, 235 in 2020, and 307 in 2021.[271] In 2022, 379 cases of euthanasia fell into this category (4.3 percent of all notifications).[272] In terms of numbers per annum, this is a record, but in terms of the percentage of all notifications, it is not.

If there is public demand for euthanasia in cases of completed life, it cannot be said, on the basis of numbers, that the Euthanasia Act was meeting it up to August 2019. However, this does not mean the Euthanasia Act cannot accommodate such demand. To determine if, and to what extent, it is able to accommodate requests for termination of "completed life," the texts of the judgments need to be reviewed. What conclusions can be drawn from these?

Up to August 10, 2019, judgments had only been published in forty-eight cases in which the due care criteria were deemed to have been complied with. However,

Table 1 Multiple geriatric syndromes

Year	Notifications based on multiple geriatric syndromes	Total number of notifications	%
2013	251	4,829	5.5
2014	257	5,306	4.8
2015	183	5,516	3.3
2016	244	6,091	4.0
2017	293	6,585	4.4
2018	205	6,126	3.3
Total	*1,433*	*34,453*	*4.2*

it has to be remembered that the researcher must make do with the sparse factual information the authors of the judgments were willing to provide under the heading "Nature of the patient's suffering," information derived mainly from documents that are not publicly available: the form completed by the coroner, the notifying physician's report, the report(s) of the consultant(s), last wills and testaments, patient records, and letters and statements from medical specialists.

However, in all published judgments, the section headed "Nature of the patient's suffering" is divided into two parts. The first part usually ends with the conclusion, "Improvement was not possible (any longer). The treatment was exclusively of a palliative nature." This part relates to the criterion's objective aspect (the suffering's hopelessness) and describes the medical condition. The second part, which relates to the aspect of unbearableness, often starts with "The suffering of the patient consisted of . . ., " and usually ends with "The patient experienced their suffering as unbearable."

In the first part, a summary is given of the illnesses and disorders that existed before the patient's death: medically classifiable illnesses and disorders such as osteoporosis, rheumatoid arthritis, decompensatio cordis, glaucoma, diabetic retinopathy, and so on; illnesses and disorders that are not life-threatening in and of themselves, and which are usually associated with advanced age. The illness(es) or disorder(s) causing the suffering is described in medical terms.

However, the authors rarely use medical terms exclusively. In the first part, terms such as "pain," "tightness of the chest," "impaired vision," "tiredness," "bedridden," "dependent on care," "limited mobility," and "loss of vitality" are almost always included as well. These terms are used to describe the direct and indirect consequences of illnesses and disorders. After all, impaired vision is a consequence of glaucoma. And being bedridden might be a consequence of severe backache, which in turn might be a consequence of osteoporosis.

It would be logical for the reported consequences (or symptoms) to be mentioned exclusively in the second part of this section. Still, very often, both the underlying disorder(s) or illness(es) and the consequences are described in the first part. Occasionally, only consequences are described in the first part, without mentioning underlying disorders or illnesses.[273] This could indicate the presence of many syndromes,[274] but it may also be unclear exactly which illnesses or disorders were involved. In that case, either the causes were not identified, or a distinction is not generally made between the illness or disorder and its consequences, as with incontinence.[275] Therefore, a certain amount of overlap usually exists between the information provided in both parts of the section "Nature of the patient's suffering" in the published rulings.

"Pain," "dependent on care," "tiredness," and "limited mobility" (factors) are also to be found in the second part of this section, in which they are used to describe the unbearable aspects of the suffering. Almost invariably, they are complemented by descriptions of circumstances contributing to the severity of that suffering.

These "aggravating circumstances" (Table 2) can relate to:

1. *The patient's biography or personality* ("the patient had always been extremely active," "the patient had always been extremely independent," "the patient . . . had always had control over their own life," "due to the character of the patient, it was impossible for her to accept the circumstances," etc.).
2. *The patient's values* ("the patient suffered because of his dependence on others," "the patient felt she was losing control over her life and that she was becoming increasingly dependent on others, something she found unaccept- able," "the patient suffered unbearably because of loss of autonomy," etc.).
3. *The patient's social circumstances* ("the patient hardly went outside," "the patient was becoming increasingly socially isolated").
4. *The patient's stamina and perspective* ("the patient suffered because of fear of further complications," "the patient did not want to go to a nursing home," "the patient did not want to go through any further loss of bodily functions").
5. *The patient's sense of purpose* ("the patient perceived her life as pointless," "the patient considered his life to be completed," "the patient . . . did not see the point of living any longer").

Pain, limited mobility, and so on were mentioned in all forty-eight cases reviewed as complying with the criteria of due care. The highest percentages of aggravating circumstances fell under the headings "Stamina and perspective" (75 percent), "Values" (56 percent), and "Biography and personality" (54 per- cent). Lack of a sense of purpose was mentioned in twenty-three judgments.

Only two judgments mentioned factors and circumstances from just one category. These judgments only referred to pain, limited mobility, and so on. The other forty-six judgments mentioned a combination of factors and circum- stances from several categories. Only two judgments referred to factors and circumstances of all categories (see Table 3).

The phrase "multiple geriatric syndromes" is somewhat misleading. The phrase suggests that if the number of medically classifiable illnesses and disorders has reached a certain level, the statutory requirement of suffering will be met. It seems to imply that there is a "tipping point," where the most recently diagnosed degenerative disorder is, as it were, the proverbial straw that breaks the camel's back and thus makes the case eligible under the Euthanasia Act.

Table 2 Reported factors and circumstances of unbearable suffering

	Pain, limited mobility, etc.	Biography and personality	Values	Social circumstances	Stamina and perspective	Sense of purpose
Number of judgments (*n* = 48)	48	26	27	22	36	23
%	100	54	56	46	75	48

Table 3 Number of reported factors and circumstances of unbearable suffering

	One category	Two categories	Three categories	Four categories	Five categories	Six categories
Number of judgments (n = 48)	2	4	10	21	9	2
%	4.2	8.3	20.8	43.7	18.8	4.2

Analysis of the published judgments reveals that the number of syndromes does not have to be high at all. Although there are indeed judgments that mention many syndromes in the first part, there are also judgments mentioning just a few. Therefore, the number of syndromes does not appear decisive: Under the "right" circumstances, just one syndrome will suffice to meet the requirement. Whether or not the suffering is "caused to a significant extent" by one geriatric syndrome will depend on the syndrome and its direct and indirect consequences, but also – and very much so – on the circumstances of the case.

5.3.2 Two Hypothetical Cases

The figures up to August 2019 do not support the claim that the Euthanasia Act already provides a "way out" for elderly people who want to have their "completed lives" ended. This does not mean, however, that the Euthanasia Act does not have the potential to provide a "way out." For the Act to be applicable, the Supreme Court stated that the suffering must be "predominantly caused by a medically classifiable (somatic or psychiatric) illness or disorder." Considering how the euthanasia review committees have applied the criterion in cases of multiple geriatric syndromes, there would seem to be much room for interpretation.

Let us explore the possibilities by considering two hypothetical cases. For example, a man of advanced age develops a severe hearing disorder because of presbycusis. He will eventually lose most, if not all, of his hearing. Medically, little can be done, and there is no way to slow down the hearing loss. The man, a former professional musician, has always lived for his music. His entire social life revolves around music. He suffers tremendously because of his deteriorating hearing. For this man, a life without music is simply inconceivable. His life will then be stripped of all meaning. The prospect of losing his hearing altogether makes him suffer unbearably, suffering which did not exist before the onset of the presbycusis. The musician, who has no other medical complaints, asks his doctor to help him commit suicide.

Does his suffering meet the requirement? Intuitively, many will be inclined to disagree since presbycusis is just one disorder commonly associated with the advancement of age. However, the circumstances of the case must also be taken into consideration. After all, properly functioning hearing is a necessary condition for this particular man's quality of life. One could argue that without properly functioning hearing his life is bereft of all quality.

Now take the hypothetical case of an elderly but healthy woman suffering from being alive. This former teacher has never been married and never had children. Furthermore, she no longer has any family, and all her friends have already died. She no longer genuinely desires to see or talk to other people. This woman is independent and healthy, but nonetheless, she is suffering tremendously under the prospect of inevitable physical and mental degeneration. She feels she has had a good life. She has managed to fulfill all her ambitions. But enough is enough, and there is no need to drag it out any longer. One day, she goes to see her doctor because of pain in her joints. The doctor tells her she has arthritis. This woman, who has no other medical complaints, then immediately asks the doctor to assist in her suicide. This case also involves just one of many frequently occurring geriatric syndromes.

The review policy of the committees indicates that one illness or disorder may suffice. The committees' reviewing practices also indicate that its impact on the patient will depend on the specific circumstances of the case. Although many will object, intuitively, to applying the Euthanasia Act in both hypothetical cases, a euthanasia review committee would likely accept the elderly musician's suffering as "caused to a significant extent by a medically classifiable illness or disorder." In his particular case, all suffering is, in a way, a consequence of the illness. Without the presbycusis, there would not have been any suffering.

But does the former teacher's suffering also meet the statutory requirement? Again, many would intuitively disagree. And not only because of the presence of merely one very common geriatric syndrome, arthritis, but presumably also because of a perceived difference in cause and consequence, which is considered somehow relevant. For this woman, life itself was already "unbearable" before arthritis occurred. Many would therefore argue that her suffering is not "predominantly caused by a medically classifiable illness or disorder." They would argue that it clearly has other, nonmedical causes. Perhaps predominantly so. Consequently, the arthritis will be seen by many as nothing but a pretext. Surely, the Euthanasia Act is not meant to justify the acts of a physician granting such a request. But would a review committee have good reasons for disapproving such action?

Of course, the musician's suffering would completely disappear if his presbycusis could somehow be cured. And, of course, even if her arthritis could be treated successfully, the teacher would continue to suffer severely. But the perceived difference between both hypothetical cases is nonsensical. The fact that, in the musician's case, all suffering can easily be linked to a medical condition, which cannot be done in the former teacher's case, makes for a rather presumptuous difference in appreciation. Are the circumstances she finds herself in less aggravating? The fact that a medical condition cannot fully explain her suffering is irrelevant because the musician's presbycusis cannot fully explain his suffering either. Both cases are similar in that respect. At first sight, many would consider the musician's case as different in some relevant way, but it does not take much reflection to learn that there is no basis for accepting such a difference in the reviewing process. There is no reason to assume that a committee would conclude that the statutory requirement was not being met in the former teacher's case. Such a conclusion would be at odds with the logic of the reviewing practice.

5.4 Some More Preliminary Observations

For a proper understanding of the way Dutch euthanasia review committees interpret the statutory requirement of suffering, and thus determine the scope of the Euthanasia Act, it is essential to realize that in their rulings on notifications involving patients with multiple geriatric syndromes, they refer to *circumstances*: facts they do not see (conceive or choose to conceive) as other causes, as causes that can be removed to eliminate the unbearableness of suffering. According to the published anonymized rulings, that is how the review committees interpret the second statutory requirement, as interpreted by the Supreme Court in its Brongersma ruling. An active lifestyle, independence, autonomy and self-control, social isolation, stamina, fear of further loss of functions, and sense of futility – all are presented as given facts by the committees in their rulings, which implies they are presented to the committees by the notifying physicians as given facts. As such, they are accepted by the committees as facts that have made the unbearableness "understandable."

Although it has not been proven yet that the Dutch Euthanasia Act provides a "way out" for elderly people intent to have their "completed lives" ended, there can be little doubt about its potential in this respect. And it should be noted that the annual number of patient requests for euthanasia based on "multiple geriatric syndromes" has risen sharply since 2019.

In a way, the KNMG 's fear of Mrs. Dijkstra's proposed new law is unfounded. All in all, there is not that much to subvert. The association itself was instrumental in shaping the review committees' policy. It did so by linking vulnerability to the medical domain, but also by allowing its various dimensions to be taken into the equation when requests for euthanasia by elderly persons are being considered. As the second hypothetical case demonstrates, it really does not take much in terms of illness or disorder for an elderly person "suffering from life" to have their suffering recognized as hopeless and unbearable, which had already become apparent as early as 2010 (see Section 5.1).

6 Concluding Remarks

Historical research will never explain conclusively why the Netherlands was the first country to decriminalize euthanasia to a considerable extent. One can only reconstruct the genesis of the Dutch Euthanasia Act. However, any such reconstruction will reveal that its rules are ultimately based on the recognition of termination of life on request and assisted suicide as acts of compassion. In the Netherlands, the decriminalization of euthanasia is not the outcome of a fundamental rights debate. It is not the result of years of struggle for more individual self-determination at the end of life. The Act has come about as a physicians' law. A doctor who has ended a patient's life does not have to fear prosecution. No criminal or disciplinary proceedings will be initiated against physicians who have observed the rules, of which only one relates to the patient's request. It is merely one of several necessary conditions that must be met.

The genesis can best be described as a growing consensus among societal stakeholders on what counts as standard and nonstandard medicine at the end of life; first and foremost, among the physicians themselves, closely followed by courts of law, and ultimately also by political parties and the legislator. In the Netherlands, termination of life on request and assisting in suicide are criminal offenses. Still, Dutch criminal courts have been willing to grant impunity to physicians who have committed those offenses by acknowledging a conflict of duties: the duty of a physician to preserve life, on the one hand, and their duty to alleviate suffering, on the other. Doctors who have felt compelled to opt for the latter at the expense of their patients' lives could successfully invoke *force majeure*. Politicians only stepped forward once societal consensus was secured. The legislator merely sealed it.

The Euthanasia Act and the practice to which its rules relate are indeed a compromise, offering something for everyone. Euthanasia is prohibited, but the law makes exceptions. There is some recognition of patient self-determination, but the decision to grant euthanasia is reserved for physicians.

Depending on perspective, compromises also can be qualified very differently. For good reasons, the Dutch euthanasia policy may be labeled liberal and progressive. Yet, the qualification "conservative" is equally appropriate. As with all hard-fought compromises, the rules agreed upon are cast in iron. Since its enactment in April 2002, the Euthanasia Act has not changed.

Dutch euthanasia policy can also be said to be emancipatory since patients can indeed ask their physicians for termination of life or assisted suicide. At the same time, it is very paternalistic. Euthanasia can only be requested by patients; it can only be asked of doctors, and requests will be granted only at their discretion.

Finally, the practice is both rigid and flexible. The statutory due care requirements have remained the same since April 2002, and there has yet to be any intention to modify them. Yet, they are open standards that allow for policymaking by the euthanasia review committees composed of nonelected experts. The statutory rules have not changed, but the committees' guidelines have.

The Euthanasia Act has been evaluated multiple times. The law is meant to provide legal certainty to physicians, assure prudent practice with regard to euthanasia by physicians, and provide an adequate framework for physicians to be accountable and for increased transparency and societal control. In these respects, according to various studies, the Act performs well. The law is considered a success.

Nevertheless, the policy is currently being challenged, first of all by those pushing for more compassion, the physicians themselves. At the behest of the medical profession, policymakers are seeking to have the Act's regulatory model applied to patients of all age groups, incompetent newborns and children included. One of the best-known arguments against the legalization of euthanasia and assisted suicide is the so-called slippery slope argument. As far back as 1958, Yale Kamisar argued that permitting termination of patients' lives at their explicit request would inevitably result in allowing patients' lives to be terminated without any such request.[276] Whatever the merits of that argument, the Netherlands did in fact introduce rules on intentional termination of life of newborns in March 2007. And, at the moment, expanding those rules to patients aged one to twelve is seriously being considered. Following the poor example set by the Supreme Court in the Coffee Euthanasia case, policymakers display a conspicuous lack of attention to fundamental rights. Seemingly, everything must yield to the physicians' desire for legal certainty. Legally speaking, policymaking in this area is approaching murky waters.

On the other hand, there is an undeniable desire for more personal autonomy at the end of life. As is shown in Section 4, euthanasia is unquestionably turning into a proper civil rights issue in the Netherlands. Currently, the Euthanasia Act's regulatory model is put forward by those advocating suicide assistance in case of a completed life. From a fundamental rights point of view, such a law would be just as unproblematic as the Euthanasia Act. The right to decide by what means and at what point one's life will end is not reserved for patients; it is an integral part of everyone's right to privacy. An act as proposed by Mrs. Dijkstra restricts the exercise of that right, as does the Euthanasia Act. And if it were to protect vulnerable persons to the same extent, it would also not be at odds with European human rights law. That law does not oblige a state to facilitate assisted suicide, but if the Netherlands were to do so in the way proposed by Mrs. Dijkstra, finding valid legal counterarguments would be very difficult.

Following the Schnabel committee's reasoning, the KNMG spoke out against the bill, not because such a law would be legally problematic, but because it would adversely affect a practice it considered to be transparent and careful. Creating a second route would be confusing and undermine existing euthanasia practice since it is likely to be circumvented. With this, the association has taken a somewhat peculiar position. It has always acknowledged the individual physician's fundamental right to decline euthanasia requests for whatever reason, whereas it apparently also feels that such requests should be addressed to physicians exclusively.

Despite appearances, a Dutch law allowing assistance in suicide in case of a completed life is not to be expected – at least, not for the time being. In the Netherlands, controversial issues are rarely regulated top-down by statute law. A bill has been introduced in parliament but has too little to build upon. As yet, too few key societal stakeholders have committed themselves. Although the current Dutch policy on euthanasia is a hard-fought compromise that took years to come about, the Euthanasia Act itself was little more than a formality. At present, Mrs. Dijkstra's law would be too great an imposition.

According to the Supreme Court's ruling in the Brongersma case, a patient's suffering must be based on a medically classifiable somatic or psychological illness to a significant extent. The regional euthanasia committees' assessment practice demonstrates that age-related conditions provide such a basis and that there is scope for nonmedical arguments as well. As early as 2010, a committee judgment showed that only a few degenerative disorders suffice. Analysis revealed that just one age-related condition would probably do. Dutch physicians will most likely accommodate completed life requests within the framework of the Euthanasia Act. In the past, physicians expanded the scope of the Euthanasia Act by deciding what kind of suffering passes as unbearable, and they will continue to do so.

Notes

Euthanasia as Privileged Compassion

1. Weyers 2004, 407–408.
2. Hoge Raad, February 8, 1944.
3. Rechtbank Utrecht, March 11, 1952; Gerechtshof Amsterdam, July 8, 1952.
4. Weyers 2004, 51.
5. Burgerlijk Wetboek (Boek 7: artt. 446–468).
6. Berg 1969.
7. Berg 1969, 47.
8. Berg 1969, 48.
9. Rechtbank Leeuwarden, February 21, 1973.
10. Rechtbank Leeuwarden, February 21, 1973; Pans 2006, 12.
11. Rechtbank Leeuwarden, February 21, 1973.
12. Rechtbank Leeuwarden, February 21, 1973.
13. Weyers 2004, 101; NVVE Over ons (Dutch Association for Voluntary Euthanasia). www.nvve.nl/over-ons/organisatie.
14. Rechtbank Rotterdam, December 1, 1981.
15. Rechtbank Rotterdam, December 1, 1981.
16. Rechtbank Rotterdam, December 1, 1981.
17. Weyers 2004, 145–146.
18. Hoge Raad, November 27, 1984.
19. Rechtbank Alkmaar, May 10, 1983.
20. Gerechtshof Amsterdam, November 17, 1983.
21. Hoge Raad, November 27, 1984; Pans 2006, 14.
22. Hoge Raad, November 27, 1984; Pans 2006, 14.
23. Gerechtshof Den Haag, June 10, 1985; Gerechtshof Den Haag, September 11, 1986.
24. Weyers 2004, 199.
25. KNMG 1984, 990.
26. KNMG 1984, 996.
27. Hoge Raad, December 15, 1987.
28. KNMG 1985, 403, 405.
29. Rechtbank Assen, April 21, 1993; Gerechtshof Leeuwarden, September 30, 1993.
30. Hoge Raad, June 21, 1994.
31. Hoge Raad, June 21, 1994.
32. Hoge Raad, June 21, 1994; Pans 2006, 16.
33. *Handelingen II* 1983/84, *Bijlage* 18331.
34. *Handelingen II* 1985/86, *Bijlage* 19359, No. 3, 2.
35. *Handelingen II* 1989/90, *Bijlage* 21132, No. 8, 47.
36. *Handelingen II* 1989/90, *Bijlage* 21300-VI, No. 22.

37. Wal & Maas 1996, 219–241.
38. *Handelingen II* 1991/92, *Bijlage* 22572, No. 3.
39. Wal & Maas 1996, 219–241.
40. *Handelingen II* 1996/97, *Bijlage* 23877, No. 3.
41. *Kamerstukken II* 1998/99, 26691, No. 2.
42. Euthanasia Act, Article 9, para. 2, sub. a.
43. Rechtbank Haarlem, July 25, 2000; Rechtbank Haarlem, October 30, 2000.
44. Gerechtshof Amsterdam, May 8, 2001; Gerechtshof Amsterdam, December 6, 2001.
45. Hoge Raad, December 24, 2002.
46. Kennedy 2002, 11–14.
47. Kennedy 2002, 11–12.
48. Kennedy 2002, 12–13.
49. Kennedy 2002, 13.
50. Kennedy 2002, 14.
51. Weyers 2004, 422.
52. *Kamerstukken II* 1998/99, 26691, No. 3, 5.
53. Burial and Cremation Act, Article 7, para. 2.
54. Burial and Cremation Act, Article 10, para. 1.
55. Burial and Cremation Act, Article 3.
56. Burial and Cremation Act, Article 10, para. 2.
57. *Kamerstukken II* 1998/99, 26691, No. 3, 6.
58. Euthanasia Act, Article 17.
59. Regionale toetsingscommissies euthanasie (Regional Euthanasia Review Committees). www.euthanasiecommissie.nl/de-toetsingscommissies/jaarverslagen.
60. Regional Euthanasia Review Committees, 2023, 9.
61. Regional Euthanasia Review Committees, 2004, 8.
62. Regional Euthanasia Review Committees, 2023, 9.
63. Regional Euthanasia Review Committees, 2023, 9.
64. Regional Euthanasia Review Committees, 2023, 11.
65. Regional Euthanasia Review Committees, 2005, 8.
66. Regional Euthanasia Review Committees, 2023, 11.
67. Regional Euthanasia Review Committees, 2023, 11.
68. Regional Euthanasia Review Committees, 2022, 11.
69. Regional Euthanasia Review Committees, 2023, 13.
70. Regional Euthanasia Review Committees, 2020, 15; Regional Euthanasia Review Committees, 2021, 15; Regional Euthanasia Review Committees, 2022, 13.
71. Regional Euthanasia Review Committees, 2023, 13.
72. Regional Euthanasia Review Committees, 2023, 13.
73. Regional Euthanasia Review Committees, 2023, 15.
74. Regional Euthanasia Review Committees, 2023, 15.
75. Regional Euthanasia Review Committees, 2023, 17.
76. Regional Euthanasia Review Committees, 2018b, 29.

77. Regional Euthanasia Review Committees, 2019, 19; Regional Euthanasia Review Committees, 2020, 19; Regional Euthanasia Review Committees, 2021, 19; Regional Euthanasia Review Committees, 2022, 15.
78. Regional Euthanasia Review Committees, 2023, 17.
79. Van der Heide et al. 2023.
80. Van der Heide et al. 2023, 287.
81. Van der Heide et al. 2023, 165.
82. Onwuteaka-Philipsen et al. 2017, 27.
83. Van der Heide et al. 2023, 165; Onwuteaka-Philipsen et al. 2017, 21.
84. Van der Heide et al. 2023, 167.
85. Van der Heide et al. 2023, 302–305.
86. Onwuteaka-Philipsen et al. 2017, 20.
87. Van der Heide et al. 2023, 292.
88. Onwuteaka-Philipsen et al. 2017, 24.
89. Van der Heide et al. 2023, 294–295.
90. Hoge Raad, April 21, 2020a; Hoge Raad, April 21, 2020b.
91. Regionale toetsingscommissies euthanasie, Oordeel 2016–85.
92. Regionale toetsingscommissies euthanasie, Oordeel 2016–85.
93. Regionale toetsingscommissies euthanasie, Oordeel 2016–85.
94. Regionale toetsingscommissies euthanasie, Oordeel 2016–85.
95. Regionale toetsingscommissies euthanasie, Oordeel 2016–85.
96. Regionale toetsingscommissies euthanasie, Oordeel 2016–85, 3.
97. Regionale toetsingscommissies euthanasie, Oordeel 2016–85, 3.
98. Regionale toetsingscommissies euthanasie, Oordeel 2016–85.
99. Regionale toetsingscommissies euthanasie, Oordeel 2016–85.
100. Regionale toetsingscommissies euthanasie, Oordeel 2016–85.
101. Regionale toetsingscommissies euthanasie, Oordeel 2016–85.
102. Dormicum is a benzodiazepine with antianxiety, amnestic, sleep-inducing, muscle relaxant, and sedative properties. Sodium thiopental is a barbiturate used for general anesthesia. It is also used as a euthanatic to put a person into a coma; to achieve this, it must be overdosed.
103. Regionale toetsingscommissies euthanasie, Oordeel 2016–85.
104. Regionaal Tuchtcollege Gezondheidszorg, Den Haag, July 24, 2018.
105. Centraal Tuchtcollege Gezondheidszorg, March 19, 2019.
106. Rechtbank Den Haag, September 11, 2019, para. 4.2.
107. Rechtbank Den Haag, September 11, 2019, para. 5.3.2.
108. Rechtbank Den Haag, September 11, 2019, para. 5.3.2.
109. Rechtbank Den Haag, September 11, 2019, para. 5.3.2.
110. Hoge Raad, April 21, 2020a; Hoge Raad, April 21, 2020b.
111. Hoge Raad, April 21, 2020a, para. 5.5.2.
112. Hoge Raad, April 21, 2020b, para. 6.5.
113. Regional Euthanasia Review Committees 2020b, paras. 4.1 and 4.4.
114. Constitution of the Kingdom of the Netherlands, Article 94.
115. Adviescommissie voltooid leven 2016, 77–91.
116. *Haas* v. *Switzerland*, para. 51.
117. *Haas* v. *Switzerland*, para. 54.

118. Buijsen 2022, 40–53.
119. Nederlandse Vereniging voor Kindergeneeskunde, 1992.
120. Gerechtshof Amsterdam, November 7, 1995; Gerechtshof Leeuwarden, April 4, 1996.
121. Overleggroep toetsing zorgvuldig medisch handelen rond het levenseinde bij pasgeborenen, 1997.
122. Overleggroep toetsing zorgvuldig medisch handelen rond het levenseinde bij pasgeborenen 1997.
123. Verhagen & Sauer 2005.
124. Chervenak et al. 2006.
125. Regeling centrale deskundigencommissie late zwangerschapsafbreking in een categorie-2 geval en levensbeëindiging bij ernstig lijden de pasgeborenen, 2007, 51.
126. Regeling beoordelingscommissie late zwangerschapsafbreking en levensbeëindiging bij pasgeborenen, 2016, Article 2.3; Review Committee on Late-term Abortions and Termination of Life in Newborns 2020 (Annual Report 2019), 2022, 15.
127. Aanwijzing vervolgingsbeslissing levensbeëindiging niet op verzoek en late zwangerschapsafbreking, 2017, Article 1.2.
128. Regeling beoordelingscommissie late zwangerschapsafbreking en levensbeëindiging bij pasgeborenen, 2016, Article 3.
129. Regeling beoordelingscommissie late zwangerschapsafbreking en levensbeëindiging bij pasgeborenen, 2016, Article 2, para. b.
130. LZA/LP&K. www.lzalp.nl/publicaties/jaarverslagen.
131. Ploem et al. 2022, 10.
132. Brouwer, Maeckelberghe, & Verhagen 2022.
133. Brouwer, Maeckelberghe, & Verhagen 2022, 10–17.
134. Brouwer, Maeckelberghe, & Verhagen 2022, 24.
135. Buijsen 2020a; Brouwer et al. 2020.
136. Ploem et al. 2022, 10.
137. Ploem et al. 2022, 125.
138. Review Committee on Late-Term Abortions and Termination of Life in Newborns 2022, 15.
139. Brouwer et al. 2019.
140. Brouwer et al. 2019, 37–40.
141. *Kamerstukken II* 2021/22, 32647, No. 92.
142. *Kamerstukken II* 2021/22, 32647, No. 92.
143. Euthanasia Act, Article 2, para. 1.
144. Regional Euthanasia Review Committees, 2013, 32.
145. Regional Euthanasia Review Committees, 2023, 11.
146. Regional Euthanasia Review Committees, annual reports. www.euthanasiecommissie.nl/de-toetsingscommissies/jaarverslagen.
147. Regionale toetsingscommissie euthanasie, Oordeel 2016-85, 14.
148. Eco 1992a, 67.
149. Eco 1992a, 67.
150. Eco 1992b, 24.

151. Eco 1992a, 78.
152. Dworkin 1986, 52.
153. Verhagen & Buijsen 2023.
154. Ploem et al. 2022, 14.
155. UN Convention on the Rights of the Child, 1989.
156. Harris et al. 2018, 206.
157. *Pretty* v. *United Kingdom*, para. 67.
158. *Haas* v. *Switzerland*, para. 51.
159. *Haas* v. *Switzerland*, para. 54.
160. *Artico* v. *Italy*, para. 33.
161. Regeling centrale deskundigencommissie late zwangerschapsafbreking in een categorie-2 geval en levensbeëindiging bij ernstig lijdende pasgeborenen, 2007, 8.
162. Vathorst et al. 2013, 104.
163. Regeling beoordelingscommissie late zwangerschapsafbreking en levensbeëindiging bij pasgeborenen, 2016, Article 3, paras. 1 and 2.
164. Aanwijzing vervolgingsbeslissing levensbeëindiging niet op verzoek en late zwangerschapsafbreking, 2017, Article 4, para. 1.
165. Regeling beoordelingscommissie late zwangerschapsafbreking en levensbeëindiging bij pasgeborenen, 2016, 8.
166. KNMG 2013, 45.
167. Optional Protocol to the Convention on the Rights of the Child on a Communications Procedure, 2012.
168. UN Convention on the Rights of the Child, 1989, Article 44.
169. Committee on the Rights of the Child, 2015, para. 28.
170. *Gard and Others* v. *United Kingdom*.
171. *Lambert and Others* v. *France*, paras. 89–95; *Gard and Others* v. *United Kingdom*, para. 83.
172. Gerechtshof Den Bosch, January 31, 2018.
173. Rechtbank Gelderland, October 22, 2013.
174. Gerechtshof Arnhem-Leeuwarden, May 13, 2015.
175. Hoge Raad, March 14, 2017.
176. Rechtbank Gelderland, October 22, 2013.
177. Euthanasia Act, Article 2, para. 1.
178. Parket bij de Hoge Raad, November 8, 2016.
179. Hoge Raad, March 14, 2017, para. 4.3.
180. Criminal Code, Article 294, para. 2 and Article 293, para. 2; Burial and Cremation Act, Article 7, para. 2.
181. Gerechtshof Arnhem-Leeuwarden, May 13, 2015.
182. Hoge Raad, March 14, 2017, para. 4.2.2.
183. Gerechtshof Den Bosch, January 31, 2018.
184. Gerechtshof Arnhem-Leeuwarden, May 13, 2015.
185. Gerechtshof Den Bosch, January 31, 2018, para. 2.3.4.
186. Gerechtshof Den Bosch, January 31, 2018, para. 2.3.4.
187. Buijsen 2018.
188. Drion 1991, 8.

189. Drion 1991.
190. Citizens' Initiative. www.tweedekamer.nl/kamerleden/commissies/verz/burgerinitiatieven/.
191. Uit Vrije Wil – Burgerinitiatief Voltooid Leven. www.uitvrijewil.nu/index.php?id=1000/.
192. Uit Vrije Wil – Burgerinitiatief Voltooid Leven. www.uitvrijewil.nu/index.php?id=1000/.
193. Uit Vrije Wil – Burgerinitiatief Voltooid Leven. www.uitvrijewil.nu/index.php?id=1000/.
194. Uit Vrije Wil – Burgerinitiatief Voltooid Leven. www.uitvrijewil.nu/index.php?id=1000/.
195. Uit Vrije Wil – Burgerinitiatief Voltooid Leven, Articles 3, 4, and 13. www.uitvrijewil.nu/index.php?id=1006/.
196. Uit Vrije Wil – Burgerinitiatief Voltooid Leven, Preamble. www.uitvrijewil.nu/index.php?id=1006/.
197. Uit Vrije Wil – Burgerinitiatief Voltooid Leven, Article 2. www.uitvrijewil.nu/index.php?id=1006/.
198. Uit Vrije Wil – Burgerinitiatief Voltooid Leven, Article 11. www.uitvrijewil.nu/index.php?id=1006/.
199. Uit Vrije Wil – Burgerinitiatief Voltooid Leven, Article 7, para. 2. www.uitvrijewil.nu/index.php?id=1006/.
200. Euthanasia Act, Article 2, para. 1.
201. *Handelingen II* 2011/2012, No. 61, 10.
202. *Kamerstukken II* 2013/2014, 32647, No. 26.
203. Adviescommissie voltooid leven 2016.
204. *Kamerstukken II*, 2013/2014, 32647, No. 26.
205. *Kamerstukken II*, 2013/2014, 32647, No. 26.
206. Adviescommissie voltooid leven 2016, 34.
207. Adviescommissie voltooid leven 2016, 36.
208. Adviescommissie voltooid leven 2016, 216–229.
209. Adviescommissie voltooid leven 2016, 216–229.
210. Adviescommissie voltooid leven 2016, 216–229.
211. Wijngaarden et al. 2020, 73.
212. *Kamerstukken II* 2019/20, 35534, No. 2.
213. *Kamerstukken II* 2019/20, 35534, No. 2, 5.
214. *Kamerstukken II* 2019/20, 35534, No. 2, 1.
215. *Kamerstukken II* 2019/20, 35534, No. 2, 5–7.
216. *Kamerstukken II* 2019/20, 35534, No. 2, 2.
217. *Kamerstukken II* 2019/20, 35534, No. 2, 2.
218. *Kamerstukken II* 2019/20, 35534, No. 2, 2.
219. *Kamerstukken II* 2019/20, 35534, No. 2, 3.
220. *Kamerstukken II* 2019/20, 35534, No. 2, 3.
221. *Kamerstukken II* 2019/20, 35534, No. 2, 8.
222. *Kamerstukken II* 2019/20, 35534, No. 2, 3.
223. *Kamerstukken II* 2019/20, 35534, No. 2, 3.
224. *Kamerstukken II* 2019/20, 35534, No. 2, 3.

225. *Kamerstukken II* 2019/20, 35534, No. 3, 19.
226. *Kamerstukken II* 2019/20, 35534, No. 3, 18–19.
227. *Kamerstukken II* 2019/20, 35534, No. 3, 19.
228. Coöperatie Laatste Wil. www.laatstewil.nu/english/.
229. Coöperatie Laatste Wil. www.laatstewil.nu/english/.
230. Kreulen 2017.
231. Akinci 2018.
232. Visser 2018.
233. Steenbergen & Dallinga 2018.
234. Steenbergen 2018.
235. Wier 2021.
236. Rechtbank Oost-Brabant, July 18, 2023.
237. Rechtbank Oost-Brabant, July 18, 2023.
238. Rechtbank Oost-Brabant, July 18, 2023.
239. Rechtbank Den Haag, December 14, 2022.
240. Rechtbank Den Haag, December 14, 2022.
241. *Kamerstukken II* 2019/20, 35534, No. 3, 33.
242. Zwanenburg 2011.
243. Regional Euthanasia Review Committees, 2011, case 11.
244. Regional Euthanasia Review Committees, 2011, case 11.
245. Regional Euthanasia Review Committees, 2011, case 11.
246. Regional Euthanasia Review Committees, 2011, case 11.
247. Regional Euthanasia Review Committees, 2011, case 11.
248. KNMG 2011.
249. KNMG 2011, 22.
250. KNMG 2011, 21–23.
251. KNMG 2011, 22.
252. KNMG 2011, 22.
253. KNMG 2011, 23.
254. KNMG 2011, 23.
255. Regional Euthanasia Review Committees, 2015.
256. Regional Euthanasia Review Committees, 2015, 31.
257. Regional Euthanasia Review Committees, 2015, 31.
258. Regional Euthanasia Review Committees, 2018b.
259. Regional Euthanasia Review Committees, 2018b, 21–22, 51.
260. Regional Euthanasia Review Committees, 2018b, 22.
261. Regional Euthanasia Review Committees, 2018b, 23.
262. *Kamerstukken II* 1999/2000, 26691, No. 6, 62; Regional Euthanasia Review Committees, 2007, 20; Regional Euthanasia Review Committees, 2018b, 23.
263. Hoge Raad, December 24, 2002.
264. Regional Euthanasia Review Committees, 2018b, 21.
265. Regional Euthanasia Review Committees, 2018b, 21–22.
266. Buijsen 2020b.
267. Buijsen 2022a.
268. Regionale toetsingscommissies euthanasie, Oordeel 2015-01.

269. Buijsen 2020b.
270. Regionale toetsingscommissies euthanasie, Oordelen 2018-44; Regionale toetsingscommissies euthanasie, Oordelen 2017-19.
271. Regional Euthanasia Review Committees, 2020, 15; Regional Euthanasia Review Committees, 2021, 15; Regional Euthanasia Review Committees, 2022, 13.
272. Regional Euthanasia Review Committees, 2023, 13.
273. Regionale toetsingscommissies euthanasie, Oordeel 2014-90.
274. Regionale toetsingscommissies euthanasie, Oordeel 2019-17.
275. Regionale toetsingscommissies euthanasie, Oordeel 2018-50.
276. Kamisar 1958.

References

Literature

Adviescommissie voltooid leven. *Voltooid leven: Over hulp bij zelfdoding aan mensen die hun leven voltooid achten.* The Hague: Adviescommissie voltooid leven, 2016.

Akinci, O. Ximena (19) kon dat zelfdodingspoeder wel erg gemakkelijk kopen. *Trouw* 10 (March 2018).

Berg, J. van den. *Medische macht en medische ethiek.* Nijkerk: Uitgeverij G.F. Callenbach, 1969.

Brouwer, M., van der Heide, A., Hein, I., et al. *Medische beslissingen rond het levenseinde bij kinderen (1–12),* 2019. https://zoek.officielebekendmakin gen.nl/blg-901797.pdf (last accessed March 23, 2024).

Brouwer, M., Maeckelberghe, E., Ten Brinke, H.-J., et al. Pediatric Brain Tumors: Narrating Suffering and End-of-Life Decision-Making. *Cambridge Quarterly of Healthcare Ethics* 29 (2020): 338–345.

Brouwer, M., Maeckelberghe, E., and Verhagen, E. *Casuïstiekbeschrijving levenseinde 1–12 jaar. Onderzoeksrapportage.* Groningen: Universitair Medisch Centrum Groningen, 2022.

Buijsen, M. A Life Fulfilled: Should There Be Assisted Suicide for Those Who Are Done with Living? *Cambridge Quarterly of Healthcare Ethics* 27 (2018): 366–375.

Buijsen, M. Commentary: Whose suffering? *Cambridge Quarterly of Healthcare Ethics* 29 (2020a): 346–353.

Buijsen, M. Uitzichtloos en ondraaglijk lijden? Over voltooide levens en gestapelde ouderdomsaandoeningen. *Tijdschrift voor gezondheidszorg en ethiek* 30 (2020b): 84–89.

Buijsen, M. Euthanasia for the Elderly: Multiple Geriatric Syndromes and Unbearable Suffering According to Dutch Euthanasia Review Committees. *Cambridge Quarterly of Healthcare Ethics* (2022a):1–9. doi: http://doi.org/10.1017/S0963180122000652.

Buijsen, M. Mutatis mutandis . . . On Euthanasia and Advanced Dementia in the Netherlands *Cambridge Quarterly of Healthcare Ethics* 31 (2022b): 40–53.

Chervenak, F., McCullough, L., and Arabin, B. Why the Groningen Protocol Should Be Rejected. Hastings Center Report 36 (2006): 30–33.

Collini, S., ed. *Interpretation and Overinterpretation.* Cambridge: Cambridge University Press, 1992.

Committee on the Rights of the Child. *Concluding Observations on the Fourth Periodic Report of the Netherlands*. Geneva: CRC, 2015.

Coöperatie Laatste Wil. Website. www.laatstewil.nu/english/ (last accessed August 30, 2022).

Drion, H. Het zelfgewilde levenseinde van oude mensen. *NRC Handelsblad* (October 19, 1991).

Dworkin, R. *Law's Empire*. Glasgow: Fontana Press, 1986.

Eco, U. Between Author and Text. In S. Collini (ed.), *Interpretation and Overinterpretation*. Cambridge: Cambridge University Press, 1992a, pp. 67–88.

Eco, U. Interpretation and History. In S. Collini (ed.), *Interpretation and Overinterpretation*. Cambridge: Cambridge University Press, 1992b, pp. 23–44.

Eco, U. Overinterpreting Texts. In S. Collini (ed.), *Interpretation and Overinterpretation*. Cambridge: Cambridge University Press, 1992c, pp. 45–66.

Harris, D., O'Boyle, M., Bates, E., and Buckley, C. *Harris, O'Boyle, and Warbrick: Law of the European Convention on Human Rights*. 4th ed. Oxford: Oxford University Press, 2018.

Kamisar, Y. Some Bon-Religious Views against Proposed "mercy-killing." *Minnesota Law Review* 42 (1958): 969–1042.

Kennedy, J. *Een weloverwogen dood: Euthanasie in Nederland*. Amsterdam: Uitgeverij Bert Bakker, 2002.

KNMG. Standpunt inzake euthanasie. *Medisch Contact* 39 (1984): 990–1003.

KNMG. Kort verslag 186ste Algemene Vergadering (I). *Medisch Contact* 40 (1985): 402–407.

KNMG. *De rol van de arts bij het zelfgekozen levenseinde*. Utrecht: KNMG, 2011.

KNMG. *Medische beslissingen rond het levenseinde bij pasgeborenen met zeer ernstige afwijkingen*. Utrecht: KNMG, 2013.

Kreulen, E. Coöperatie Laatste Wil vindt poeder voor vrijwillig levenseinde. *Trouw*, September 1, 2017. https://bit.ly/49inF5C (last accessed March 25, 2024).

Nederlandse Vereniging voor een Vrijwillig Levenseinde. Website. www.nvve.nl/over-ons/organisatie (last accessed August 20, 2022).

Nederlandse Vereniging voor Kindergeneeskunde. *Doen of laten? Grenzen van medisch handelen in de neonatologie*. Utrecht: NVK, 1992.

Onwuteaka-Philipsen, B., Legemaate, J., Evenblijk, K., et al. *Derde evaluatie Wet toetsing levensbeëindiging op verzoek en hulp bij zelfdoding*. The Hague: ZonMw, 2017.

Overleggroep toetsing zorgvuldig medisch handelen rond het levenseinde bij pasgeborenen. *Toetsing als spiegel van de medische praktijk.* Rijswijk: Overleggroep toetsing zorgvuldig medisch handelen rond het levenseinde bij pasgeborenen, 1997.

Pans, E. *De normatieve grondslagen van het Nederlandse euthanasierecht.* Nijmegen: Wolf Legal Publishers, 2006.

Ploem, M., Krol, E., Asscher, E., et al. *Evaluatie Regeling beoordelingscommissie late zwangerschapsafbreking en levensbeëindiging bij pasgeborenen.* The Hague: ZonMw 2022.

Steenbergen, E. van. Laatste Wil stopt definitief met verspreiden dodelijk poeder. *NRC Handelsblad,* March 26, 2018.

Steenbergen, E. van, and Dallinga, M. OM onderzoekt coöperatie om dodelijk poeder. *NRC Handelsblad,* March 21, 2018.

Uit Vrije Wil – Burgerinitiatief voltooid leven. Website. www.uitvrijewil.nu/ index.php?id=1000/ (last accessed August 30, 2022).

Van der Heide, A., Legemaate, J., Onwuteaka-Philipsen, B., et al. *Vierde evaluatie Wet toetsing levensbeëindiging op verzoek en hulp bij zelfdoding.* The Hague: ZonMw, 2023.

Vathorst, S. van de, Gevers, J., Heide, A. van der, et al. *Evaluatie Regeling centrale deskundigencommissie late zwangerschapsafbreking en levensbeëindiging bij pasgeborenen.* The Hague: ZonMw, 2013.

Verhagen, E., and Buijsen, M. Should the Dutch Law on Euthanasia Be Expanded to Include Children? *Cambridge Quarterly of Healthcare Ethics* 32 (2023): 5–13. https://doi.org/10.1017/S0963180122000457.

Verhagen, E., and Sauer, P. The Groningen Protocol – Euthanasia in Severely Ill Newborns, *New England Journal of Medicine* 352 (2005): 959–962.

Visser, M. Coöperatie Laatste Wil maakt werk van zelfdodingspoeder. *Trouw,* February 9, 2018.

Wal, G. van der, and Maas, P. van der. *Euthanasie en andere beslissingen rond het levenseinde.* The Hague: Sdu, 1996.

Weyers, H. *Euthanasie: Het proces van rechtsverandering.* Amsterdam: Amsterdam University Press, 2004.

Wier, M. van de. OM: zeker vijftien mensen overleden na aankoop middel X bij Alex S. *Trouw,* October 21, 2021.

Wijngaarden, E. van, Thiel, G. van, Hartog, I., et al. *Perspectieven op de doodswens van ouderen die niet erg ziek zijn: de mensen en de cijfers.* The Hague: ZonMw, 2020.

Zwanenburg, E. Toetsing euthanasie stilzwijgend versoepeld. *Medisch Contact* 66 (2011): 2128–2130.

Treaties, Laws, Regulations, and Instructions

Treaties

Convention for the Protection of Human Rights and Fundamental Freedoms, Rome, November 4, 1950 (ETS No. 005).

Optional Protocol to the Convention on the Rights of the Child on a Communications Procedure 2012, New York, December 19, 2011.

UN Convention on the Rights of the Child, New York, November 20, 1989. www.ohchr.org/en/instruments-mechanisms/instruments/convention-rights-child (last accessed March 25, 2024).

Laws

Burgerlijk Wetboek (Boek 7: artt. 446–468), *Stb.* 1991, 600 [*Civil Code, Book 7, Articles 446–468*].

Grondwet voor het Koninkrijk der Nederlanden, *Stb.* 1840, 48 [*Constitution of the Kingdom of the Netherlands*].

Wet op de lijkbezorging, *Stb.* 2014, 380 [*Burial and Cremation Act*].

Wet toetsing levensbeëindiging op verzoek en hulp bij zelfdoding, *Stb.* 2001, 194 [*Euthanasia Act*].

Wetboek van Strafrecht, *Stb.* 1886, 6 [*Criminal Code*].

Regulations

Regeling centrale deskundigencommissie late zwangerschapsafbreking in een categorie-2 geval en levensbeëindiging bij ernstig lijden de pasgeborenen, *Stcrt.* 2007, 51 [*Regulation Establishing the Central Expert Committee for Category-2 Late-Term Abortions and Termination of Life in Newborns*].

Regeling beoordelingscommissie late zwangerschapsafbreking en levensbeëindiging bij pasgeborenen, *Stcrt.* 2016, 3145 [*Order Establishing the Review Committee on Late-Term Abortions and Termination of Life in Newborns*].

Instructions

Aanwijzing vervolgingsbeslissing levensbeëindiging niet op verzoek en late zwangerschapsafbreking, December 1, 2017, *BWBR0040270* [*Instruction on the Prosecution of Termination of Life Not on Request and Late-term Abortion*].

Parliamentary Proceedings and Parliamentary Papers

Proceedings

Handelingen II 1983/84, *Bijlage* 18331.
Handelingen II 1985/86, *Bijlage* 19359, No. 3.
Handelingen II 1989/90, *Bijlage* 21132, No. 8.
Handelingen II 1989/90, *Bijlage* 21300-VI, No. 22.
Handelingen II 1991/92, *Bijlage* 22572, No. 3.
Handelingen II 1996/97, *Bijlage* 23877, No. 3.
Handelingen II 2011/2012, No. 61.

Papers

Kamerstukken II 1998/99, 26691, No. 2.
Kamerstukken II 1998/99, 26691, No. 3.
Kamerstukken II 1999/2000, 26691, No. 6.
Kamerstukken II 2012/2013, 31036, No. 7.
Kamerstukken II 2013/2014, 32647, No. 26.
Kamerstukken II 2019/20, 35534, No. 2.
Kamerstukken II 2019/20, 35534, No. 3.
Kamerstukken II 2020/21, 32647, No. 82.
Kamerstukken II 2021/22, 32647, No. 92.

Case Law

European Court of Human Rights

Artico v. *Italy.* European Court of Human Rights, May 13, 1980, App. No. 6694/74.

Gard and Others v. *United Kingdom.* European Court of Human Rights, June 27, 2017, App. No. 39793/17.

Haas v. *Switzerland.* European Court of Human Rights, January 20, 2011, App. No. 31322/07.

Lambert and Others v. *France.* European Court of Human Rights, June 5, 2012, App. No. 46043/14.

Pretty v. *United Kingdom.* European Court of Human Rights, April 29, 2002, App. No 2346/02.

Supreme Court of the Netherlands

Hoge Raad, February 8, 1944, *NJ* 1944,314.
Hoge Raad, November 27, 1984, *NJ* 1985,106.

Hoge Raad, December 15, 1987, *NJ* 1988,811.
Hoge Raad, June 21, 1994, *NJ* 1994,656.
Hoge Raad, December 24, 2002, *NJ* 2003,167 (ECLI:NL:HR:2002:AE8772).
Hoge Raad, March 14, 2017 (ECLI:HR:2017:418).
Hoge Raad, April 21, 2020a (ECLI:NL:HR:2020:712) (criminal case).
Hoge Raad, April 21, 2020b (ECLI:NL:HR:2020:713) (disciplinary case).
Parket bij de Hoge Raad, November 8, 2016 (ECLI:NL:PHR:2016:1086).

Court of Appeal

Gerechtshof Amsterdam, July 8, 1952, rolnr. 524/1952.
Gerechtshof Amsterdam, November 17, 1983, *NJ* 1984,43.
Gerechtshof Den Haag, June 10, 1985, *NJ* 1987,608.
Gerechtshof Den Haag, September 11, 1986, *NJ* 1987, 608.
Gerechtshof Leeuwarden, September 30, 1993, *TvGR* 1993/62.
Gerechtshof Amsterdam, November 7, 1995, *NJ* 1996/113.
Gerechtshof Leeuwarden, April 4, 1996, *TvGR* 1996/15.
Gerechtshof Amsterdam, May 8, 2001, *ELRO* AB1474.
Gerechtshof Amsterdam, December 6, 2001, *LJN* AD6753.
Gerechtshof Arnhem-Leeuwarden, May 13, 2015 (ECLI:NL:GHARL:2015:3444).
Gerechtshof Den Bosch, January 31, 2018 (ECLI:NL:GHSHE:2018:345).

District Court

Rechtbank Utrecht, March 11, 1952, *NJ* 1952,275.
Rechtbank Leeuwarden, February 21, 1973, *NJ* 1973,183.
Rechtbank Rotterdam, December 1, 1981, *NJ* 1982,63.
Rechtbank Alkmaar, May 10, 1983, *NJ* 1983,407.
Rechtbank Assen, April 21, 1993, *TvGR* 1993/42.
Rechtbank Den Haag, September 11, 2019 (ECLI:NL:RBDHA:2019:9506).
Rechtbank Haarlem, July 25, 2000, beschikking art. 250 Sv, parketnr. 15/035127-99.
Rechtbank Haarlem, October 30, 2000, parketnr. 15/035127-99.
Rechtbank Gelderland, October 22, 2013 (ECLI:NL:RBGEL:2013:3976).
Rechtbank Den Haag, December 14, 2022 (ECLI:NL:RBDHA:2022:13394).
Rechtbank Oost-Brabant, July 18, 2023 (ECLI:NL:RBOBR:2023:3640).

Disciplinary Board

Centraal Tuchtcollege Gezondheidszorg, March 19, 2019 (ECLI:NL:TGZCTG:2019:68).
Regionaal Tuchtcollege Gezondheidszorg Den Haag, July 24, 2018 (ECLI:NL:TGZRSGR:2018:165).

Review Committee on Late-Term Abortions and Termination of Life in Newborns

Annual Reports

Review Committee on Late-term Abortions and Termination of Life in Newborns 2020. *Annual Report 2019*. Utrecht: LZA/LP, 2022.

Annual reports are available at www.lzalp.nl/publicaties/jaarverslagen/ vertalingen.

Regional Euthanasia Review Committees

Annual Reports

Regional Euthanasia Review Committees. *Annual Report 2003*. The Hague: Regional Euthanasia Review Committees, 2004.

Regional Euthanasia Review Committees. *Annual Report 2004*. The Hague: Regional Euthanasia Review Committees, 2005.

Regional Euthanasia Review Committees. *Annual Report 2006*. The Hague: Regional Euthanasia Review Committees, 2007.

Regional Euthanasia Review Committees. *Annual Report 2010*. The Hague: Regional Euthanasia Review Committees, 2011.

Regional Euthanasia Review Committees. *Annual Report 2012*. The Hague: Regional Euthanasia Review Committees, 2013.

Regional Euthanasia Review Committees. *Annual Report 2017*. The Hague: Regional Euthanasia Review Committees, 2018a.

Regional Euthanasia Review Committees. *Annual Report 2018*. The Hague: Regional Euthanasia Review Committees, 2019.

Regional Euthanasia Review Committees. *Annual Report 2019*. The Hague: Regional Euthanasia Review Committees, 2020a.

Regional Euthanasia Review Committees. *Annual Report 2020*. The Hague: Regional Euthanasia Review Committees, 2021.

Regional Euthanasia Review Committees. *Annual Report 2021*. The Hague: Regional Euthanasia Review Committees, 2022.

Regional Euthanasia Review Committees. *Annual Report 2022*. The Hague: Regional Euthanasia Review Committees, 2023.

Annual reports are available at https://english.euthanasiecommissie.nl/the-committees/annual-reports.

Codes of Practice

Regional Euthanasia Review Committees. *Code of Practice*. The Hague: Regional Euthanasia Review Committees, 2015.

Regional Euthanasia Review Committees. *Euthanasia Code 2018*. The Hague: Regional Euthanasia Review Committees, 2018b.

Regional Euthanasia Review Committees. *Euthanasia Code 2020*. The Hague: Regional Euthanasia Review Committees, 2020b.

Codes of Practice are available at https://english.euthanasiecommissie.nl/the-committees/code-of-practice.

Regional Euthanasia Review Committee Judgments

Regionale toetsingscommissies euthanasie, Oordeel 2012-04.

Regionale toetsingscommissies euthanasie, Oordeel 2012-18.

Regionale toetsingscommissies euthanasie, Oordeel 2012-21.

Regionale toetsingscommissies euthanasie, Oordeel 2012-42.

Regionale toetsingscommissies euthanasie, Oordeel 2014-90.

Regionale toetsingscommissies euthanasie, Oordeel 2015-01.

Regionale toetsingscommissies euthanasie, Oordeel 2016-85.

Regionale toetsingscommissies euthanasie, Oordeel 2017-19.

Regionale toetsingscommissies euthanasie, Oordeel 2018-44.

Regionale toetsingscommissies euthanasie, Oordeel 2018-50.

Regionale toetsingscommissies euthanasie, Oordeel 2019-17.

Judgments are available (in Dutch) at www.euthanasiecommissie.nl/uitspraken-en-uitleg.

Acknowledgments

I am indebted to all who have sharpened my thoughts on Dutch euthanasia policies and practices while writing this Element. As always, Erasmus University Rotterdam provided me with a wonderful environment in which to work. I am particularly grateful to the members of its health law department, with whom I have had many discussions over the years on the subject of euthanasia: Caressa Bol, André den Exter, Mai Fleetwood-Bird, Eva Földes, Ernst Hulst, Ageeth Klaassen, Eline Linthorst, Philipa Mos, Marjolein Simonis, Lujia Sun, and Marjolein Timmers. When one has colleagues who are so well-informed and talented, work is as much a pleasure as it is instructive.

I also thank Cambridge University Press, particularly Julia Ford and Vidya Ashwin Krishnan, for their many helpful suggestions for improvement.

Tomi Kushner, who came up with the idea for this Element, has been unwavering in her commitment. She has contributed in more ways than one, and I am forever in her debt.

Cambridge Elements ☰

Bioethics and Neuroethics

Thomasine Kushner

California Pacific Medical Center, San Francisco

Thomasine Kushner, PhD, is the founding Editor of the *Cambridge Quarterly of Healthcare Ethics* and coordinates the International Bioethics Retreat, where bioethicists share their current research projects, the Cambridge Consortium for Bioethics Education, a growing network of global bioethics educators, and the Cambridge-ICM Neuroethics Network, which provides a setting for leading brain scientists and ethicists to learn from each other.

About the Series

Bioethics and neuroethics play pivotal roles in today's debates in philosophy, science, law, and health policy. With the rapid growth of scientific and technological advances, their importance will only increase. This series provides focused and comprehensive coverage in both disciplines consisting of foundational topics, current subjects under discussion and views toward future developments.

Cambridge Elements ⹀

Bioethics and Neuroethics

Printed in the United States
by Baker & Taylor Publisher Services